The Hou

Summertime, and the emigrant workers, dressed in new suits and dreams, are returning home for the annual sojourn. They are young, vigorous; they have money in their pockets. But they do not belong here any more – and they do not belong abroad. They are resentful, dangerous. None more so than the seemingly gregarious Christy Cavanagh. His childhood fixation with Mrs de Burca and her daughters moves into frightening obsession when he finds that the date has been set for the auctioning of their house.

Tom Murphy has received numerous awards and honours. His awards include the Irish Academy of Letters Award, the Harveys Irish Theatre Award (twice), the Sunday Tribune Arts Award, the Independent Newspapers Theatre Award, the Sunday Independent/Irish Life Award, the Drama-Logue Critics Award and the Irish Times/ESB Theatre Award. He also holds honorary degrees from the University of Dublin (Trinity College) and NUI (Galway).

Tom Murphy was born in Tuam, County Galway, and now lives in Dublin.

by the same author

On the Outside (*with Noel O'Donoghue*)
A Whistle in the Dark
A Crucial Week in the Life of a Grocer's Assistant
The Orphans
Famine
The Morning After Optimism
The White House
On the Inside
The J. Arthur Maginnis Story
The Vicar of Wakefield (*from the novel by Oliver Goldsmith*)
The Sanctuary Lamp
Epitaph Under Ether
(*compilation from the works of J. M. Synge*)
The Blue Macushla
The Informer (*from the novel by Liam O'Flaherty*)
Conversations on a Homecoming
Bailegangaire
A Thief of a Christmas
Too Late for Logic
The Patriot Game
The Gigli Concert
She Stoops to Folly
(*also from Oliver Goldsmith's* The Vicar of Wakefield)
The Wake
The Seduction of Morality (*a novel*)

The House

Tom Murphy

Methuen Drama

Published by Methuen 2000

1 3 5 7 9 10 8 6 4 2

First published in the United Kingdom by
Methuen Publishing Limited
215 Vauxhall Bridge Road
London SW1V 1EJ

Methuen Publishing Limited Reg. No. 3543167

A CIP catalogue record is available from the British Library

ISBN 0 413 75790 0

Typeset by Deltatype Ltd, Birkenhead, Merseyside
Printed and bound in Great Britain by
Cox & Wyman Ltd, Reading, Berkshire

Introduction

In Lorrie Moore's wonderful novel *Who Will Run the Frog Hospital?*, an American man is discussing the 1960s with his younger wife. 'We made the sixties,' he says. 'We made the counterculture. You were twelve years old.' 'But,' she replies, 'we inherited it and as children we made ourselves around it, with it . . . The counterculture got on the ground floor with us, as children; it was the wood we were built with.' The husband is having none of this. 'But it was still ours. It came from inside of us, not you.'

In Ireland the counterculture of the 1960s ran deeper, unfolded at a slower pace and took longer to become the new orthodoxy. It was made, essentially, not by hippies or anti-war protestors, but by writers: John McGahern, Edna O'Brien, Brian Friel, John B. Keane, Thomas Kilroy, and, of course, Tom Murphy. They broke open an old world, an inherited structure of language, emotion and aspiration with the force of anger, realism, youth, and sex. And they invented a new one, articulating on page and stage a universe of rage, loss, desire and hope that was at first so strange to the governing orthodoxy as to be literally unrecognisable as Irish.

When Tom Murphy sent his great first full-length play, *A Whistle in the Dark* to the Abbey, the managing director Ernest Blythe informed him that there were no such people as he had depicted.

These writers were almost all the children of small-town Ireland. The new culture they articulated came from within those places and within themselves. But very slowly and very painfully, over a period of at least 20 years, it came to belong to the rest of Ireland as well. Almost everyone who grew up here in the 1960s, 1970s, and 1980s inherited it. It was the wood they were made with.

For those who are now in their 20s, 30s and 40s, it was the material out of which they made themselves. As time went on it became so much a given, so taken for granted, as to be almost invisible. What came from inside these writers is now all around us. It is the cultural air we breathe every day and think about as little as we think about breathing.

This is why a writer like Tom Murphy remains so vital, and why it is so fascinating that he has been revisiting, as he does in his new play at the Abbey, *The House*, the small-town world of the 1950s. By some crass standard of 'relevance', in a culture obsessed with novelty, that world may seem dead and gone. In a society struggling to cope with immigration, what meaning can a play like *The House*, steeped in the psychic disruptions of emigration, possibly have? In a society awash with the neuroses of new wealth, isn't it just a cop-out for the National Theatre to be presenting plays set in an impoverished past?

But the great function of theatre as a public art has always been to utter, in one form or another, the words 'on the contrary'. It is always at its most vital when it goes against the grain.

The suffocating orthodoxy of the 1950s was that nothing mattered except tradition. The rage that powered the great theatrical explosion of the early 1960s was an overwhelming need to contradict the smug assumptions and give expression to a reality that had no place within them. Now, the suffocating orthodoxy is that the new Ireland came from nowhere, that nothing matters except our present state of ironic, free-floating post-modernity. We should be grateful that Tom Murphy still has the energy to contradict it.

Murphy, in any case, has never been a mere product of small-town pre-1960s Ireland. Much of his best work has been set in other times and places. *Famine* filters the repressions of 1950s Ireland through the trauma of the 1840s. *Bailegangaire* suspends that world between, on the one hand, a dislocated 1980s Ireland in which the local multinational electronics factory is about to close and, on the other, a baroque, pre-modern, folkloric culture.

The Sanctuary Lamp and *The Gigli Concert* unfold in different kinds of urban religious space with heroes who are not even Irish. *Too Late for Logic* travels through middle-class Dublin. *The Morning After Optimism* takes place in a fairytale forest.

Murphy, too, is not merely a great Irish dramatist, but a great European one. His imagination, from the very start, has been fabulously cosmopolitan. Far from being stuck in a provincial corner of a marginal society, he has re-animated the common heritage of European myth. Faust hovers over *The Gigli Concert*, Orpheus over *Too Late for Logic*, Oedipus over *The Sanctuary Lamp*.

Even what might be regarded as his most acutely sociological and most viscerally political play, *A Whistle in the Dark*, is, in its form, a perfect Greek tragedy. Even the most apparently traditional setting in Murphy's work, the rustic cottage of *Bailegangaire*, has a kind of reverse relationship with a modern European myth, George Orwell's *1984*. While Orwell imagined a world in which everyone was being watched, Murphy's play, also set in 1984, gives us, as he told Nicholas Grene – whose book, *The Politics of Irish Drama*, was published recently by Cambridge University Press – 'lives that no one is watching'.

But what makes him one of the half-dozen great living dramatists in the English language is that he has eluded the apparent alternatives. Lesser playwrights have to choose whether to be realists or poets, myth-makers or social realists, excavators of a given patch of ground or wide-ranging explorers. Murphy is always both at the same time. The mythic pitch of his stories and the linguistic arias of his dialogue go hand-in-hand with a precise and penetrating sense of society.

And often, that society has been a version of his native Tuam. From *On the Outside* in 1959 through *A Crucial Week in the Life of A Grocer's Asistant*, *The White House*, *Conversations on a Homecoming*, *The Wake* and now *The House*, there is a kind of inner history of the place he grew up in. The language, the snobbery, the striving, the jokes and tragedies of a single town run like a seam of ore beneath Murphy's work.

What's crucial, though, is that this sense of place is also, all the time, a state of displacement. Nothing could be more wide of the mark than to imagine Murphy now as an ageing writer in a radically altered Ireland being drawn back for comfort to the familiar world of his youth. For the whole point of that world is that it is never, ever, familiar.

Murphy seems genetically incapable of nostalgia, but even if he were inclined to drift back to a lost wholeness, a bygone community in which everything fitted together and everything made sense, he couldn't do it. His Tuam has always been deeply and fundamentally fractured. 'Home', in Murphy is a place that does not exist unless it is invented.

The reason, simply, is emigration. Murphy's Tuam is quite literally inconceivable without the presence of an elsewhere, for elsewhere is where so many of its people live. When he imagines the place it is always through the eyes of someone returning from England or America or even, in the case of *A Whistle in the Dark*, actually in exile. And exile, in Murphy, is not just a matter of location. It is a condition so fundamental that it has seeped into the bones of those who stay as much as those who go. It shapes family, friendship, personality, even dreams. It becomes the human condition itself.

Far from diminishing with distance, this sense of disturbance only becomes stronger. The backward glance becomes even more ferocious. In *The House*, the return to the 1950s is not a nostalgic trip down memory lane, but a voyage to the roots of a deep unsettlement.

At a psychological level, 1950s Tuam is ground zero for Murphy's explosive emotion. At a sociological level, it is the worst of modern times, a period when emigration and its psychic consequences were at their height. What you get in *The House* is, in fact, the precise opposite of nostalgia: a vision of the past that, instead of releasing us from the present, confronts us with the forces that shaped it.

To go back to Lorrie Moore's paradigm, what Murphy does is to transform what is now outside us in 21st century Ireland back into what it felt like when it was inside us. Few cultures are so fortunate as to have their creators still around, undercutting their smugness, contradicting their assumptions, bringing the forces that made them back into play.

Fintan O'Toole
This article first appeared in the *Irish Times* in April 2000.

for johnny

The House

The House was first presented at the Abbey Theatre, Dublin, on 12 April 2000. The cast was as follows:

Mother	Geraldine Plunkett
Marie	Jane Brennan
Christy	Patrick O'Kane
Louise	Deirdre Molloy
Jimmy	Gary Lydon
Peter	Andrew Bennett
Goldfish	Don Wycherley
Bunty	John Olohan
Kerrigan	Frank McCusker
Susanne	Ali White
Tarpey	Des Cave

all the other roles were played by

Paul Keeley	Fergal McElherron
Fiona Kelly	Geoff Minogue
Maeve Leonard	Daithi O'Suilleabdhain

Director   Conall Morrison
Set Designer   Francis O'Connor
Costume Designer   Joan O'Clery
Lighting Designer   Ben Ormerod
Stage Director   Finola Eustace
Voice Coach   Andrea Ainsworth
Fight Director   Richard Ryan

Characters

Mother (Mrs de Burca)
Marie
Christy
Louise
Jimmy
Peter
Goldfish
Bunty
Kerrigan
Susanne
Tarpey
Extras (to play returned emigrants, sympathisers . . .)

Setting

1950s Ireland

Scene One

Mother and **Marie** *have had lunch at their garden table (beneath a tree). July.* **Mother** *is a TB convalescent. One shoulder is lower than the other perhaps (due to a collapsed lung).* **Marie** *is in her thirties. (She's tall, perhaps, and angular.) A hint of spinsterhood.*

Mother *sips from a glass of Guinness and grimaces, not savouring it.*

Marie   'It's good for you.' (*They share a smile.*)

Mother   . . . Glorious! (*The day.*) . . . Thank you, love, thank you. (*For the lunch.*) . . . We'll miss our tree.

Marie   Oh, I don't know. The advantages of living in the town?

Mother *nods, as to herself, in the slow, formal manner: a characteristic.*

Marie   I saw what looked like really nice ham in McCabe's window and I'll get some for this evening and we'll have it with a salad.

Mother   Thank you, love . . . Glorious!

Marie   . . . There's someone coming up the drive . . . Mum, you have a visitor.

Mother   I have? Who?

Marie   Christy Cavanagh.

Mother   Christy?! Our lovely gentle boy. 'I'd like to be this family please.'

Christy (*off*)   Lovely day!

Marie   Lovely day.

Mother   Christy! (*Rising.*)

Christy (*coming in*)   Don't get up, Mrs de Burca!

Mother   Christy, Christy, my dear, my dear!

Christy   How're you all, how are you, Mrs de Burca?

She takes his two hands, kisses him. She would kiss him again but it might embarrass him.

He's twenty-nine or thirty, handsome, with a touch of masculine rawness. New suit, quality of its kind, though it would appear that he's a builder's labourer. Forties–fifties film star influence.

There's an unusual bond of affection and ease between him and Mrs de Burca. By contrast, he is self-conscious of **Marie** *– and she of him. She disapproves of him, he feels (wrongly; in fact, it's the contrary). And she's older than him.*

Mother   My dear! – Now! – How are you?

Christy   Terrific! (*A nod:*) Marie. (*And wonders should he shake hands/kiss her/which. And, clumsily, does neither. He offers to assist* **Mother** *back to her chair.*) Here, let me give you a . . . You're feeling well again?

Mother   Thank you, thank you. (*She's seated.*) Now! Home again for the summer!

Christy   Home again for the summer! – (*And laughs:*) As usual!

Mother   As usual!

Christy   As usual, Mrs de Burca! How're things, Marie?

Marie   Fine, thank you.

Christy   All right, yeh?

Marie   Yes.

Mother   When did you arrive?

Christy   This morning early.

Mother   On the boat.

Christy   On the boat.

Marie   Sit down?

Christy   Thank you. On the boat, Mrs de Burca, the *Princess Maud*, cattle boat, crowded, the lot of us from Holyhead. The train before that, eight hours of it, just as bad, packed from Euston Station. I hit the sack as soon as I got in and only woke up half an hour ago. (*Celebratory:*) The scenery! Isn't it a lovely day, what!

Mother   Isn't it absolutely glorious!

Christy   Glorious, Mrs de Burca, absolutely!

Marie   Would you like some tea?

Christy   No thanks, Marie.

Mother   Christy?

Christy   No thanks.

Marie   I can make some fresh.

Christy   Amn't I grand now here!

Marie *takes the tray of lunch things off to the house.*

Mother   Thank you, love. And how are things at home?

Christy   Home? (*Momentarily puzzled. Here, de Burcas' place, is 'home' to him – at least subconsciously.*)

Mother   Your father.

Christy   Oh! (*And laughs:*) Isn't the aul bastard old now so what more damage can he do anyone! (*He indicates the lawn:*) Hay must be fetching a great price this year, Mrs de Burca?

Mother *laughs.*

Christy   How long since that lawn saw a lawnmower? I was looking at it all the way up the drive.

Mother   Tommy Smith, who was doing it for us, emigrated too last spring.

Christy   Is Timmy gone too? There'll soon be no one left. Well, it never looked like that when I used to do it. But you're keeping well again?

Mother   Not too bad now. (*And on second thoughts:*) Yes!

Christy   And McGreedy, where is Mrs McGreedy?

Mother   She died.

Christy   Aw! I knew there was something, coming in the gate, when I didn't hear her bark.

Mother   And is everything all right with you, Christy?

Christy   Oh yes, oh yes!

Mother   Plenty of work?

Christy   Plenty of it!

Mother   On the buildings?

Christy   On the, on the – (*He takes out his cigarettes to fidget with them.*) Closed down now over there of course for the annual two weeks. The changes that's happening over there: there'll be building work going on in England for the next twenty years, Mrs de Burca.

Mother   But you'll stay home for the rest of the summer.

Christy   Oh I'll stay – As usual! Oh I'll stay, let the others go back after their two weeks – let them off, off with them! But I'll take my cue from the swallows.

Mother   Give me one of those.

He looks at her: should she be smoking?

Give me one of those.

Christy (*gives her a cigarette, lights it*)   And how is Susanne?

Mother *holds up a clenched fist:* **Susanne** *would appear to be a handful.*

Christy (*laughing, disagreeing*)   No! No! Still at the secretarial?

Mother   Yes. I believe so.

Christy   Still in London?

Mother   Still in London.

Christy   I haven't seen Susanne now for . . . Or, I was in a place over there one night and I'd nearly have sworn it was her I saw, but when I got the chance to look around again she was gone. And that she spotted me. But hardly: it was hardly

Susanne's kind of place, if you know what I mean.

Mother   She'll be home on Friday.

Christy   Susanne will?

Mother (*nods.*)   She's fine. And Louise is . . . (*Unease. Then:*) All fine. And your brothers, Christy, where are they?

Christy   Scattered, somewhere, I do believe.

Mother   And do you ever see them?

Christy (*dismisses the matter as of no consequence to him. Then, silently:*)   Oh! Something for you. (*An object from his pocket.*)

Mother   What is it?

Christy   Hang about. (*It's a pendant and, in the manner of a child playing with a toy aeroplane, he goes:*) Z-z-z-z-z-z . . . ! (*And he presents it to her.*)

They have a great laugh. It's a crucifix and chain.

Mother   Just what I needed: a crucifix!

Christy   Glorious! (*The place, the day. Then:*) Oh! (*He has something else for her: a story.*) Yeh know Robin Hood, Mrs de Burca?

Mother   I do.

Christy   Your man with the feather, bow and arrow, Sherwood Forest?

Mother   Yes.

Christy   Well, he's dying. Aw he's very bad. And he's in bed in his bedroom. And he says to his friend the friar who's with him: Friar, pull back them curtains, open that window so that I may behold my beloved Sherwood Forest for one last time. And the friar does what he's told. Now, says Robin Hood, hand me down my bow and arrow. And he gets them. Now, says he, aiming the bow – the hands are shaky on him. But, he says, wherever this arrow is to fall it's on that spot that I'm to be buried by my merry men. And he fires. And d'you know where they buried him? On top of the wardrobe.

They have another laugh, together with:

Stupid! Stupid!

Mother   Well, God bless you, Christy!

Christy (*celebratory of the place and day again*)   But this place will never change. Absolutely!

Mother   We're selling.

Christy   ... You're?

Mother's *characteristic nod.*

Christy   *Here?*

Mother   We're on the move too.

As best he can he is concealing his shock. He would like to ask why are they selling but **Marie** *is returning. She has her car keys and a glass of lemonade, which she puts on the table.*

Marie   Time for your rest now, Mum.

Mother   Look at the lovely present Christy brought me.

Marie   What is it?

Mother   Dakka-dakka-dakka-dakka-neeavachchah-z-z-z-z-z-z ... (*Aeroplane starting up, taking off on a runway ...*)

Marie *to* **Mother**'s *side to assist her, if required, out of her chair.* **Mother** *takes a folded newspaper that is on the table.*

Mother   I'll manage now. Sit for a while, Marie, and talk. (*A bow:*) Christy.

Christy   Mrs de Burca.

Mother *goes off to the house.*

Christy   That – flipping – grass is annoying me. And rushes down there near the gate. When rushes get out of hand, tck! (*Looking in a new direction – a shock:*) What happened to the wall?

Marie   What?

Christy   Look! The wall! That's a *party* wall between here and your man's: a whole section of it is down.

Marie   It – fell?

Christy   To be looking out on that'd depress anyone.

Marie   D'you want a lift back to town?

Christy   What? No. The walk. I'll go back by the wood and the river. Is this for me? (*The lemonade.*)

Marie   Yes.

Christy   And the drive is gone totally gammy. I'm surprised you've a spring left in your car. Does the lawnmower work, is there oil, petrol – a mix – in the shed?

Marie   I don't know, I expect so.

Christy   I'd do it now but – (*His good suit.*) I'll give it a lash tomorrow. What? Will I?

Marie   As you please.

Christy   If you think that's all right?

Marie   Well, call.

Christy (*silently?*)   What?

Marie   Mum loves seeing you. Well. (*She prepares to go.*)

Christy   Oh! (*He has a present for her. He offers it:*) Actually.

Marie   For me?

Christy   Well! (*Meaning, if she doesn't want it.*)

Marie   No! (*She accepts the little parcel.*)

Christy   It's only a – (*He shrugs.*)

Marie   Thank you.

He shrugs.

I have to go back and reopen the shop.

Christy   Of course.

Marie   My assistant is on holidays ... Well.

She leaves, annoyed with herself (frowning at her self-consciousness of him) and without opening the present (which is a handkerchief or small silk scarf.)

Her car driving away. **Christy** *with his lemonade, wondering about this new situation, the lights fading a little. (Passage of time.)*

Another car, this time arriving. It stops, the engine is left running. **Louise** *will enter in a moment. She is in her middle twenties, youthful and curvaceous in a summer dress. (There has been a relationship between them, now unsatisfactory to him.)*

Louise *(off)*   Fancy a spin? *(Coming in:)* It's only me – I heard you were back – Isn't it a lovely day! – How yeh!

Christy   How are you?

Louise   Fine, fine – *now*. How are *you*, which is more important?

Christy   Yeh know!

Louise   The suit. Isn't it a lovely day?

Christy   Terrific, terrific! Everything all right, then?

Louise   Yeh! No, I heard you were back with the rest of the returning – exodus – and since I was passing your house I called there, just in case you might be at a loose end so to speak – wanderlust – and when there was no one there I knew – of course! – this had to be your first port of call – How are you?

Christy *(gestures that he's fine. Then:)*   Your mother is looking – *(Gestures 'fine'.)*

Louise   Terrific! Well, not too bad now. She's resting, I suppose?

Christy   Yeh.

Louise   I'm on my way to Newcastle: I've stuff to pick up there before the shops close, but we could take our time on the way back? Meander?

Christy   The walk.

Louise   I understand: You've been travelling. Ooh!

Lemonade. Home-made! Did Marie make this for you? (*She has a sip from his glass. Then:*) So, when shall we two meet again? Tonight.

Christy   Aw –

Louise   Stop.

Christy   I don't know –

Louise   Ah stop, stop.

Christy   Louise –

Louise   Stop.

Christy   And you shouldn't call at my place.

Louise   There was no one around to see me – I wouldn't have called if there was! Your father's truck or anyone!

Christy   No –

Louise   No, no, no! (*A quick look around, then her arms around him to kiss him:*) Oh gosh-golly it's fantastic to see you, you're looking fantastic, I cried for days when you went back last year, I nearly died. And you never wrote.

Christy   I never said I'd –

Louise   But I forgive you. Come in the back way to our place tonight before closing time – No, Christy! Scruples, that's all you're talking about: *I* don't have them! Scruples are – scruples!

Christy   Louise –

Louise   This? (*Her wedding ring. Mouths it:*) Shite! Him? (*Her husband. Mouths it:*) Shite! And you'll give in to me in the end!

He rolls his eyes / sighs / whatever. A handful of coins from his pocket to poke a finger through them to find his present for her: earrings.

What did you bring me?

Christy   Your mother is selling here.

Louise   Quick, I have to dash.

Christy   Why is she selling?

Louise (*accepting the earrings*)   Ooh!

Christy   What's the problem?

Louise (*shrugs; she isn't interested.*)   They aren't new. They're lovely, but they aren't new. *Where* do you come by these things? See you tonight? – See you tonight. You're looking fan-tastic.

And she's gone. He stands there. Her car driving away. And, after a moment, he leaves too, with a problem to be resolved.

Scene Two

Goldfish, **Peter** *and* **Jimmy** *are drinking in* **Bunty**'s *bar/back bar/snug. (At a remove from them are* **Kerrigan** *and* **Tarpey**, *discussing business.* **Tarpey** *in police inspector's uniform. They will leave shortly.) Night.*

Goldfish *has a gold watch, a gold ring – like a knuckle-duster – and a moustache, after a film star (Cesar Romero?). He is returned from America: his dress and vocabulary tell the story. (He is short, perhaps, and disproportionately broad-shouldered.) A lot of energy – he moves like a boxer – and he is given to drumming violent rhythms on the counter. (His attitude promises the violent development of the story.)*

Peter *is forty-ish. Essentially a simple soul, an innocent. He is returned from England and he has a bastard accent and a petrol-blue mackintosh with epaulettes to prove it.*

And **Jimmy** *is in his thirties, a local who has not gone home from work. He is in a boiler-suit. In drink he's a know-all. His attitude to the returned emigrants is supercilious (the way he laughs at/mimics their accents) and envious (because of his own situation and the rolls of money they flash).*

Jimmy   You're wrong!

Peter   Naw! –

Jimmy   You're wrong! –

Peter   I'm not, Jimmy –

Jimmy   You don't know the first thing you're talking about!

Peter   But, Jimmy, like, England!

Jimmy   Bull!

Peter   But all I'm saying is –

Jimmy   Yes, and you're wrong! Talk sense! Isn't there rationing all the time over there sure!

Peter   Naw! –

Jimmy   Yes!

Peter   Steak! Twice a week! If you know the runs to the right diggins.

Kerrigan *and* **Tarpey** *are leaving.*

Jimmy   Inspector Tarpey, Mr Kerrigan!

Goldfish   Now we can all relax. Long arms o' the law is leavin'.

Kerrigan *is gone.* **Tarpey** *hangs back.*

Goldfish   'Spector Dick Tracy, always gets his man – or child.

Tarpey *leaves.*

Goldfish   Yup, Pedro! (*'You were saying'*)

Peter   You understand what I'm talking about, Goldfish.

Goldfish   Man?

Peter   Bob's your uncle!

Goldfish   . . . Fanny's yer aunt?

Peter   That's what I'm saying! I had to leave here same as everyone else. England, Jimmy, you gets a living over there, fair fucking doos like.

Jimmy   Oh now, that's Churchill talking.

Peter   Ay?

Jimmy   The big cigar on him.

Goldfish   'Down ol' Kentucky where ho'shoes is lucky.' (*Singing it to no one.*)

Peter   See them! (*His teeth.*) Top and bottom. (*Double dentures.*) Wife's the same. You walk in, the other side, there's no one is looking down their noses [as] much as to say 'Look what's coming in the door'. It's your right like, Bob's your uncle, they kit you out with all the teeth you want. For free. Even if y'are who y'are. Black or white. Ay?

Goldfish   All the pearly choppers – huh? – yeh want.

Jimmy   Karl Marx!

Peter   Ay?

Jimmy   The Welfare State: sure all that's there for sure is for the spreading of communism!

Peter   Naw!

Jimmy   The nuns they're raping every week all over the world!

Goldfish   'See the village smithy standin' –'

Peter   I go to Mass every Sunday!

Jimmy   I couldn't disagree with you more!

Goldfish   Simon! (*Calling for service.*)

Peter   Well, take a gloak at these. (*Producing pay packets for Jimmy's inspection.*) I was working down the road there where you're still working, Jimmy, and what was I drawing home?

Jimmy   Oh, I'm a chargehand down there now.

Peter   Fiver a week. Two pounds for the mother, three pounds for booze and fuck-all for myself.

Goldfish (*beats a drum roll; then, calls*)   Simon!

Jimmy   Look it! – (*Returns the pay packets.*) – a straight answer, Peter: do you love your country?

Peter   Ay?

Jimmy   Declare your allegiance, or do you have an anchor at all, at all?

Peter (*to* **Goldfish**)   Ay?

Goldfish   Your anchor, man: Mutiny on the Bounty?

Peter   ... I love my country! Here, mate! This land! And I do dream about it and all.

Jimmy   Listen to him.

Goldfish   And you listen to *him*. (*Speaking it rapidly and to no one in particular:*) 'See that village smithy standin' neath that thare ol' ches'nut tree' man!

Peter (*now laughing*)   I love my country above my king, Goldfish!

Goldfish   These guys here is talking Peruvian!

Christy *comes in and gives a whoop.*

Christy   Whee-hee!

Jimmy   Oh-ho look in, the hard!

Goldfish   Hee-haw!

Peter   Aw Jesus Christ, Khrisht, heigh-up, mate!

Jimmy   Put it there, me aul segoasha!

Christy   Peter, Jimmy! Martin! (**Goldfish***'s proper name.*)

Goldfish   Chris! Chris! Goddammit! Man!

Peter   Good to be home, Khrisht, ay?

Christy   Yeh! –

Goldfish   Jesu Christu, kid! Put up them dukes! (*Mock pugilistics, clenching ...*)

Jimmy   'Jesu Christu goddammit!'

Christy   Get up those steps! (*Boxing.*)

Goldfish   Git him on the downstairs!

Peter   Good to be home like!

*And **Bunty** (proper name Simon) is coming in (behind the counter). He's fifty-ish, round, busy in speech and movement. **Peter** signalling to him to set up another round.*

Peter   Bunty! –

Goldfish   I love yeh, Baby! –

Peter   What're y'having, mate! –

Bunty   You're welcome, Christy, son! –

Jimmy   'I love yeh, Baby!'

Christy   What's the news, Simon?

Bunty   News, Christy? – I wouldn't know where to begin! –

Peter   Same again, Bunt, and whatever Khrisht is having like!

Goldfish (*wants to buy the round*)   Nanty-up, Pedro! Your poison, kid? –

Jimmy   What's the whore-master having – I'm getting this one –

Goldfish   Stall, man –

Peter   My round –

Jimmy   'Stall, man – my round – we makes money round here too like, heigh-up, mate – oo-aw – know what I mean like!' On the slate, Simon.

Bunty   You're all right there now, Jimmy, your mother with the tea on the table waiting on you [for] the last four hours. Custom of the house, custom of the house, first drink – (*He gives a brandy to **Christy**.*) Now, Christy, son, the same as I give everyone else – first drink of the season for the emigrants is on me, and the last when ye're all off again in a few weeks' time and we're all glad to see the backs of ye. Now, am I to start filling another round or what?

Goldfish   Set 'em up, Joe!

Christy   When 'd you get in?

Goldfish   Toosday!

Jimmy   The Boston burglar!

Christy   Plane?

Goldfish   Wild blue yonder!

Peter   You get in this morning, Khrisht?

Christy (*'yeh'*.)   You, Peter?

Peter   Yesterday.

Goldfish   We gotta make some plans! –

Peter   And the missus like –

Goldfish   Gotta do few things! –

Peter   She's English.

Christy   Yeh?

Jimmy   And the 'kiddies', Peter?

Peter   Ow-aw. (*'Yes'*)

Goldfish   Git us some action 'n' excitement!

Bunty (*filling/serving drinks*)   News, men? – No, I wouldn't know where to begin. Sylvester Keane? – Died poor fella. Did ye hear? – Yeh.

Peter   Sylvester like?

Bunty   Forty-two. Mary Devine the Old Road? This afternoon. I only heard it in there [a] while ago myself. Lord have mercy on the soul of the – And come here to me, Sylvester's little sweetshop up for sale already in the newspaper: I'll be auctioning it for his missus next week, the creature.

Christy   Did he leave her badly off, Simon?

Bunty   That's another matter. Judge Costello – Remember him? Remains taken to the church [a] few hours ago. Party of them in there now and out here (*front and back bars*) all evening coming from the funeral, including 'the man who got there', your old friend and neighbour one time, Christy, Billy Kerrigan.

Goldfish   The DA.

Bunty   Yeh, that's the way it goes.

Christy   Is Billy Kerrigan out there now?

Bunty   No, he was there, you just missed him: left while ago with Inspector Tarpey.

Goldfish   Dick Tracy.

Bunty   We're in the County Final – Did ye hear? Yeh, the Juniors. De Burcas' place down in Woodlawn – where you used to work one time, Christy? – I have the selling of that too. Here, it's all in here, local paper, the *Sentinal* – what's on in the pictures, Stephanie Roche's recipes for how to boil an egg, ads and all the details of the auctions – I'm only wasting my time talking. (*He has put the local paper on the counter.*) Now, with yere big wads of money, which one of ye is paying for that round because though I'm a poor man I'm a busy one.

Goldfish   Stall, Pedro. (*As he gets his money.*)

Bunty   But de Burcas' place'll be a nice place for someone.

Peter   And set up my round, Bunty, mate.

Bunty (*going off*)   Haven't you only one mouth on yeh, Peter?

Goldfish   Yo-o! (*His toast.*)

Jimmy   Fair play t'yeh, Goldfish!

Peter   Men!

Christy   Cheers!

They drink. **Christy** *takes up the local paper, folds it/rolls it up, possessively.*

Jimmy   Yeh married or anything, Goldfish?

Goldfish   Few times. Guess I durn't darn recall 'xactly. (*Which they find funny.*)

Christy   Give us a hand with a bit of a wall in a day or two?

Goldfish   Sure thing. You, Jem-boy, married or anything?

Jimmy   Married – Me? – Naaw! I'm like Gregory Peck here. (*Christy.*) We know where to get it for free.

Goldfish   Yeah?

Jimmy   The married ones! Up on your bike, Cavanagh!

Christy   Saturday be all right? (*To mend the wall.*)

Goldfish   Sure thing. (*To Jimmy.*) Yeah?

Jimmy   Married women!

Peter   Yeh like?

Jimmy   And they're broke-in for you sure – Oi, Christy? – and there's safety in them: they can't hold you responsible for nothing.

Goldfish   Ride 'em cowboy!

Jimmy   'Oo-aw!'

Bunty (*returning with change for **Goldfish***)   Tom Egan the Dublin Road? On his way out too they tell me, poor fella – Now, Goldfish. (*Change.*) Yeh, TB.

Peter   There's people dying now that never died before.

They laugh.

Bunty (*moving off*)   That's the way it goes.

They drink.

Christy   But how's it cuttin' anyway?

Goldfish   Yih gits a bit o' a kick outa the blacksmith blues!

*Which they find very funny. And they drink again. And **Louise** comes in, some paper money in her hand.*

Peter   Bunty! (*Calling for service for her.*)

Louise   Welcome home!

Peter   Ma'am!

Jimmy   Mrs Burgess! (*Arch.*)

Bunty (*returning*)   Louise?

Louise   D'you have change, Simon?

Bunty   Ye're busy down there? (*Taking her money.*)

Louise   Fairly. There's crowd from the funeral and the lads back from England of course.

Bunty   The latchycoes! (*Going off again.*)

Christy   How many kids, Peter? (*Self-consciously, he had turned his back on Louise.*)

Peter   Two, Khrisht.

Christy   Yeh?

Peter   They're above at home now with the mother, and the missus. She's English like.

Christy   Yeh, you were saying.

Jimmy   Get them off yeh! (*An undertone, sexual innuendo to do with **Louise**.*)

Christy   You're in where, Peter?

Peter   Well, I'm on the move like but Brum, Birmi'ham I go back to. Steel-fixin', with me mate like, Davy, Davy Johns, yeh know, he's a Taffy like, and we travels all over. (*He gives his pay packets to **Christy**:*) Ay?

Jimmy   Steel-fix that! (*Innuendo as before.*)

Christy   That's good money.

Peter   Fair ol' touch, ay? MacAlpine, Laing, Higgis and Hill – we works for them all. Wimpey, Gallaghers, William Moss.

Jimmy   Ay! (*As before.*)

Peter   And smashing bloke and all, Davy, me mate like, yeh know. I mean, for a Taffy like, for a Welshman.

Bunty (*returned with change*)   Now, Louise: I'm low on the two-bobs but it's near closing time and that should see you through down there.

Louise   Thanks.

Bunty   You're welcome, you're welcome. (*He's gone again.*)

Louise   Goodnight!

Peter   Goodnight, ma'am!

Jimmy   Mrs Burgess!

Louise *leaves.*

Jimmy   Bow-wow, bow-wow!

Peter   Fine thing that like.

Jimmy   A good night's lodgings there, boys – Goldfish, Christy?!

Peter (*starts to sing*)   'I is for the Irish in your –'

Jimmy   'I is for the Irish in your tiny heart, my dear' – Jesu Christu! ('*Oops!*')

Jimmy, *on his last – 'Jesu Christu!' – moving to go out to the gents, has staggered and a heavy drunken hand on* **Goldfish** *to steady himself. Big violence potential: for a moment it looks as if* **Goldfish** *is going to head-butt or hit* **Jimmy**, *but he contains himself. Instead:*

Goldfish   Harriet, you are a fool! (*A Bette Davis accent and line.*)

Jimmy   Y'have lovely teeth, Cavanagh!

Christy (*contains himself also. Smiles*)   No provoke! (*In a Spanish accent; probably a line from a film.*)

Jimmy   And! Peter! Cardinal Mindszenty! They're torturing him, aren't they? See?! In Hungary! So where's your anchor, where d'you belong? Lads, ye belong nowhere, ye belong to nobody. (*Going out.*) 'I is for the Irish in your . . .'

Momentarily sobering. But now, **Goldfish** *beats a drum roll in celebration of his hatred and the near violence, and Bette Davis again – And they laugh.*

Goldfish   Harriet, I have never made a practice of slapping people but I am dangerously close to it now!

Christy (*returns pay packets to* **Peter**)   Good money, Peter – I is for the Irish.

Peter (*singing*)   'In your tiny heart, my dear/R means right and when you're right you have no need to fear/E is for Eileen, your mother's name I mean/And L is for the lakes where I first met my own colleen.'

Goldfish   Hee-haw! (*And another drum roll.*)

Peter   'Then A is for the angels that are watching over you/ N means never frown.'

Goldfish/Peter/Christy   'Keep smiling through.'

Goldfish   Hee-*fucking*-haw! (*Harsh laugh and drum roll.*)

Peter   'And D is for your Daddy's lesson.'

Goldfish/Peter   'And I hope 'twill be a blessin'.'

Christy   Simon!

Peter/Goldfish   'That's how I spell Ireland!'

The lights fading. **Christy** *indicating to* **Bunty**, *who is off, another round; another drum roll from* **Goldfish**, *this one silently;* **Christy** *stroking the local paper.*

Scene Three

Later. **Kerrigan**'s *house. (Kitchen.)* **Kerrigan** *is in his shirt-sleeves, working on some documents. A glass of water nearby him. The doorbell rings, he's mildly surprised, he answers it.*

He's in his thirties. He's a solicitor. He has a private practice and he is also a State Solicitor. (A regional prosecutor, a type of DA.) His voice is mock-gruff. He's proud of himself. He likes a compliment. He's a likeable man.

Kerrigan Oh?

Christy Billy!

Kerrigan The hero is back! *(Returning with Christy:)* Be the hokies has to be the thing to say! Home is the hero, the swallow, golondrina, St Christopher the traveller, come in, you're welcome, yes, at this delightful hour of the night, sit down! If we can find a chair for you that doesn't bear the marks of the children's ... What did I tell you? *(The last on discovering a child's dirty nappy on the seat of a chair. He picks it up gingerly and dumps it.)* These things are all over the place. A drink you're looking for, I suppose, brandy you're drinking, I suppose – Good man!

Christy Am I disturbing you?

Kerrigan Are you disturbing me, you are disturbing me but I was nearly finished anyway. *(He's tidying away his documents.)* I had to leave the office early to go to a funeral, Judge Costello's, and I had to take a look at these for the morning.

Christy How was it?

Kerrigan The funeral? Dead. But I had to be there and be *seen* to be there. Oh I can perform my role too, though lately risen from the lower orders. Show my now august presence as another fierce and fearless upholder of the laws of the land like the good judge himself, and he was only a bollix – Sit down.

Christy *(sits. Perhaps he is fingering the local paper that he carries.)*   A car crash I heard.

Kerrigan Yes. He was drunk of course, but of course that couldn't come out, seeing as who he was. The state of this country: hypocrisy, discrimination, mediocrity: Disgraceful. They don't know, they don't care! And there's no honesty or brains left in it, except my own. How's your father?

Christy   Ah yeh. How're the kids?

Kerrigan   Bundles of joy: can't you see the state of the place! (*And a few sniffs at the air, as to detect evidence of more dirty nappies.*)

Christy   And Sheila?

Kerrigan   Another bundle of joy! She's worn out, the creature, she tells me. (*Papers tidied away, he has found two glasses and a gin bottle containing some gin.*) Now, is this brandy good enough for you? And I had the mixers here already waiting for you. (*The glass of water. He sits.*)

Christy   No, the house is grand.

Kerrigan (*pouring drinks*)   Hm?

Christy   But if you wanted to do a bit of touching-up to the paintwork?

Kerrigan   No.

Christy   Or anything! Because I'll be a free agent now for a while.

Kerrigan   No thanks, you're very good. Well, *nunc est bibendum*!

Christy   Cheers, mate!

They drink.

But.

Kerrigan   What?

Christy (*shrugs/shakes his head. He has a hidden agenda, but how to introduce it. Then:*)   Jays, you've come a long way, Billy, you've some head on yeh.

Kerrigan   I'll have some head on me, my friend, in twenty-five years' time when the mortgage is paid off. Are you making money?

Christy, *a clownish villain, expressing 'maybe I am'.*

Kerrigan   What? (*Chuckling.*)

Christy (*same clown*)   By all means possible, Billy!

Kerrigan   And you'll blow it all in a week or two like all the other Paddies back from England. You will! It amazes me: holding up pub counters every year here, day and night. You will! Why can't you! (*Be wise/have sense. Quieter.*) And get out of Barrack Street. Like me. Show them. Like me.

Christy   Yeh, I agree. But.

Kerrigan   What?

Christy   I heard Sylvester Keane died, poor fella.

Kerrigan   He did, he did, poor Sylvester, he did. Forty-two?

Christy   Yeh, Bunty was telling us.

Kerrigan   Bunty! Now *there's* an example for you! What must he have been up to in England to come home after only six or seven years away and buy that pub – outright! – in High Street? What?! Sure he must have been doing some unmerciful fiddling.

Christy   He's some musician all right.

Kerrigan (*laughing, enjoying the wit*)   Aw God! (*Then:*) I hate him.

Christy   And, I see in the paper here, Sylvester's little sweetshop is up for sale already?

Kerrigan   'Tis. Was there trouble down town?

Christy   No.

Kerrigan   But there will be. Three seasons of the year it's like a graveyard round here, summer it's the Wild West. What?

Christy   Tombstone! (*They laugh.*) And I see de Burcas' place down in Woodlawn is up for sale too.

Kerrigan   'Tis. I'm handling the legal side of that sale.

Christy (*nods. He has read it in the paper*)   And are *they* in trouble? Is that why they're selling – are they broke or what?

Kerrigan   Hmm?

Christy   What would that place go for?

Kerrigan   Which, the sweetshop?

Christy *nods*.

Kerrigan   Oh, it won't make the nine. Eight hundred, thereabouts, would be my guess. I won't be far wrong.

Christy   And de Burcas'?

Kerrigan   Woodlawn?

Christy *nods*.

Kerrigan   Hard to say.

Christy   I mean, what's its value? I mean, if they had the money, if they had its value, would that keep them going, living there?

Kerrigan *frowning*.

Christy (*shrugs*)   Would there be a reserve price on that place?

Kerrigan   There would. And are they in trouble, are they broke or what and why are they selling is none of your business either. And while I'm on the subject of the de Burcas, Christy, leave Michael Burgess's wife alone.

Christy *agrees – clownish – that's what he would like/wants to do*.

Kerrigan   She's a married woman.

Christy   Yeh. (*Soberly*.)

Kerrigan   Why don't you put your feet on the ground? What has that family got to do with you? Why don't you settle down? You're making money, you say – if you are – and find some *ordinary* kind of woman?

Christy   Who?

Kerrigan   One that hasn't too much of anything. D'you know what I mean? I never trusted extremes.

Christy Who?

Kerrigan Who?! A maiden then, a virgin!

Christy Where would a man start looking for one of them?

Kerrigan Aren't they all over the place! If we're to believe Mother Church. And I believe in the efficacy of Mother Church's teachings.

They are laughing. **Kerrigan** *puts a finger to his lips: not to awaken Sheila and the children upstairs. (And he has talked himself out of his alertness of a few minutes ago.)*

And between you, me and the wall – I'm only marking your card for you – Mrs Burgess, 'Louise', is no good. Chocolate sweets and pricks. And you're not the first one there, from what *I* hear. (*He tops up the drinks, lal-lawing a line from the song 'La Golondrina':*) Lal-lal-lal-law, lal-lal-lal-lal-lal-law, lal-lal-lal-law! It's hard to say, you know, with those big old places, *difficile dictu*. They'll be all right now with two-three. (£*2,300.*)

Christy Is that exact?

Kerrigan They'd be more than happy, I'd say, with two-four, two thousand four hundred. That'd be my guess.

Christy Cheers, mate! (*And he sits back.*)

Kerrigan I know they were good to you one time, or whatever it was they did, but – (*He touches his forelock*) – thank ye kindly for that now, God bless ye: Forget it. I'm sure it made them feel virtuous, as it does their kind. But they're an odd bunch. Even the so-called steady one, Marie, the chemist. Still waters there, my friend, running very deep. Normans! Norman blood sure from way back: it never left them. They never fitted in here – D'you know what I mean? They're – different. Good luck! (*He is about to drink, he sniffs the air.*) D'you get it? New house, yes, but the smell of children's shit in here is something terrible.

Christy *laughs. And, now,* **Kerrigan** *begins to laugh at himself. The laughter getting out of control:* **Kerrigan**'s *finger to his lips – wife and children upstairs. The laughter subsiding, the lights fading.*

Scene Four

De Burcas'. Saturday.

Off, single, sharp, cracking sounds (like rifle fire): heavy stones being dropped, one on the other. A wall is being built. And celebration of the hard work.

Goldfish (*off, singing*)   'Oh they're tough, mighty tough in the West/They got lumps of curly hair upon their chest –' (*And, as a man lifting a heavy stone:*) Whee-hee-hup! (*And dropping it on a wall:*) Down, you basta'd! Hee-haw!

*While **Mother** is arriving at the garden table to put a book on it (photograph album), to take out a handkerchief to cough, but contains the cough: **Peter** is coming in, as from a tap at the rear of the house, with two buckets of water.*

Without stopping, he nods/smiles 'Ma'am' to her. She nods, smiles. Then – his politeness, gentleness – he stops.

Peter   It's a nice day?

Mother   It is, a nice day.

And he's gone.

Goldfish (*off*)   Hey, Pedro, man, mosey! One hour ahead o' the posse, the buff-shams is hot on our trail – Whee-hee-hup! Down, you basta'd!

*While **Mother** coughs into her handkerchief. She stops because voices are coming from the house. **Louise** and **Susanne** are coming to join her.*

Susanne *is barefooted and in a silk-ish type of dressing gown that hangs open over something flimsy. She is in her late twenties. She has a mug of tea. She's self-centred, self-absorbed, self-conscious, vulnerable. But she puts on an act. She mainly only listens to herself, she exaggerates, she appears to want arguments/discussions both ways. There is some kind of rage in her – or is it hurt? Both! And there is a sense of futility. But she puts on an act.*

Louise   And is the car new?

Susanne   *Good* morning, *good* morning!

Mother   Good *morning*!

Susanne   Mother! And how are we today?

Louise   Morning? It's one o'clock in the day.

Mother   I sent Louise up to you with the tea.

Susanne   Right!

Mother   And not miss the lovely sunshine.

Susanne   Right! Heaven! I can smell the grass.

Louise   The lady of leisure.

Susanne   I can hear the river.

Goldfish (*off*)   Whee-hee-hup!

Susanne   Who are they?

Louise   Christy Cavanagh.

Goldfish (*off*)   Down, you basta'd!

Mother   Christy and some 'mates'. (*She likes the word.*) Did you sleep well?

Susanne   So-so. Like a log! What are they doing?

Mother   Mending the wall. The rain brought it down.

Susanne   Such furious activity.

Mother   Yes.

Christy (*off*)   Peter, put a bit over here!

Mother   Such a waste! Those strong boys having to go away.

Susanne   And me. Aa sure now, I'm a poor emigrant too.

Louise   You didn't *have* to go away.

Susanne (*has sat with her tea and to pick at her toenails*)   Well, who has come to view the house?

Mother   Oh.

Susanne   How many?

Mother Some. And there have been enquiries, I believe. I asked Marie to get us some coffee for you and we'll be having lunch shortly when she arrives.

Susanne I couldn't eat a thing, Mum.

Mother Just something light.

Susanne Amn't hungry, Mum.

Mother Love?

Susanne Moth-er!

Louise I can't stay to lunch.

Mother Because we won't be eating again 'til half-seven.

Susanne Right! How much do you pay him?

Mother Christy? He'd be offended.

Susanne Would he? (*She knows better.*)

Mother Yes ... 'I'd like to be this family please.' That's what he said to me once. His mother used to bring him down here with her, in her – *basket*. Then, as an infant, *toddling* along beside her. And then, when she died, he started to come down here on his own, a little soul. And he arrived one day with his *bundle*: 'I'd like to be this family please' ... And I'd have taken him in, properly, to live here, had him educated, instead of half-measures. But there was no way of talking to that father of his: a mule. A mule, a *mule*! But I *should* have. Instead of half doing it.

Goldfish (*off*) Christy! Give's a hand with this Moby Dick! ... Whee-hee! – (*Two men lifting a stone.*)

Christy } Hup! ... Down, you basta'd!
Goldfish } Hup! ... Down, you basta'd! ... (*And laughter.*) Hee-haw!

Mother They're working too hard. Boys, boys! You're working too hard! (*Going off to join them:*) Take a rest! We'll be having something to eat, shortly ...

Peter (*off*)   Not at all, ma'am . . . (*Indistinguishable conversation.*)

Susanne (*to no one*)   Who is he? What is he? What does he *want* of us all these years?

Louise   He's the real thing.

Susanne   Has he been sniffing around you since he came home?

Louise   What d'you mean?

Susanne (*to no one*)   Heathcliff. (*Then:*) Oh, come on – Baby! Standing there like someone in a romantic agony. You should spend a few years abroad and you'll find out! You should – There's more than one of you in the world, you know!

Louise   I don't know what you're talking about.

Susanne   You know he's a pimp, don't you?

Louise   *What* are you talking about?

Susanne   Tea! (*She doesn't like tea.*) They're all pimps. People try to use people. They *try*. But they do not get very far with me. People would walk on you – literally.

Louise   As a matter of fact he hasn't even looked at me since he came home.

Susanne   People in this town think we're stupid. Why is she so soft? Mum. He's a servant boy. (**Christy** *is.*) Has anyone come to view the place? Do you trust auctioneers? Tierney, that fat little person with the pub – Bunty. And his wife like Humpty Dumpty's mother. Do you trust anyone? And meanwhile, Mr Bunty is acquiring half the town for himself. Well, we shall see about that.

Louise   . . . You're daft.

They react to **Marie**'*s car, which is arriving.*

Susanne   And Marie, efficiency, intelligence. She would let the grass grow under her feet. Though I'm sure she thinks otherwise. This family is gone to the dogs. Honestly, every time I come home I get depressed.

Marie (*off*)   Afternoon!

Susanne   Afternoon! (*To no one:*) All men are pimps. (*To* **Marie**, *who is coming in:*) Sister!

Marie   The wall is coming on. Sleep well?

Susanne   Yes!

Louise   Is that a grey hair, Susanne?

Susanne   Stop!

Louise   A cluster – a colony of them – Marie, look!

Susanne   Gedoutofit!

Marie   I didn't see your car properly in the dark last night when you arrived: is it new?

Louise   That's what I was asking.

Susanne   It's a car. A car? A little thing, a Fiat? A car, for God's sake!

Marie (*laughing*)   Where *do* you get the money? (*To* **Mother**, *who is about to enter:*) Newspaper!

Mother   Thank you, love.

Susanne   A present then, if you must know. (*To no one.*)

Marie   And I got some ice cream.

Mother   Yippee.

Christy, **Peter** *and* **Goldfish** *are in tow.*

Marie   Afternoon.

Christy   Marie, Louise.

Mother   Did you see the wall?

They are looking off at the wall.

Peter   Nice stone. It'll be nice all right.

Mother   It is nice stone.

Peter   We're putting a bit of concrete in the middle: it won't show but it'll keep it together like.

Christy   It won't come down so fast again in a hurry. Susanne, welcome home!

Susanne   Hm? (*Has he addressed her/has someone noticed her?*)

Mother (*to herself*)   You're bringing the place back to life. Now, boys, come over here.

Christy   All right, yeh? (*To* **Susanne**.)

Susanne   Yes.

Mother   Lunch will be ready in a jiffy. This is Susanne.

Peter   Ma'am!

Susanne   Gentlemen master builders! (*She vacates the table: could be she doesn't want to sit with anyone, could be she is flaunting herself in scant attire.*) It's a cavity wall then!

Christy   Ah no. ('*That's ridiculous.*' *Politely.*)

Susanne   But would it not be more effective in concrete blocks?

Peter   Aw God, no.

Susanne   But some of those granite stones must weigh a ton.

Marie   Surely limestone.

Susanne   Still!

Peter   Bit of exercise for us like, keep down the old gut, ay?

Susanne   Or a ha-ha?

They don't know what she's talking about.

Mother (*pointed*)   Susanne, are you going to get dressed, love? Boys! (*Calling them to the table.*)

Peter   We're grand, ma'am.

Mother   Won't you have something to eat?!

Susanne (*to no one*)   But I expect you know best. (*About building a wall.*)

Christy   Martin? (*'Something to eat?'*)

Goldfish *shakes his head: this is not at all his scene.*

Peter   We got the nod from the gaffer here, ma'am: [to] go across the fields to the Halfway House: drop Coco-Colo to wash down the dust.

Marie   Some sandwiches, Mum, when they come back.

Peter   Twenty minutes then, Khrisht. (*To* **Goldfish***:*) We can get out this way.

Peter *and* **Goldfish** *leave.*

Mother   Christy! (*Calling him to the table.*)

Christy   And the secretarial? (*To* **Susanne***.*)

Susanne   Yes!

Marie   Are you staying to lunch?

Louise   I can't.

Marie *to the house.* **Mother** *opening photograph album.*

Mother   We were looking at these last night when Susanne arrived and there are one or two here of your mother.

Christy   Staying long, Susanne?

Susanne   We shall see.

Mother   There she is. Isn't it? (*A photograph.*)

Christy *nods, looking at the photograph, while off:*

Goldfish (*off, in the distance, laughing, singing*) 'Don't take your guns to town, son, leave your guns at home, Bill, don't take your . . . '

Louise   A bicycle of one of our customers was stolen from the yard last week. (*She's feeling spare, left out of it.*)

Mother   What is the world coming to? (*Still looking at the photograph:*) She was a great help to me. And friend.

Susanne Oh well, I suppose I *had* better go to my workbench: put on my make-up.

Mother Do, love, and don't waste the day.

Christy Susanne.

Susanne (*to* **Louise**) Ciao! (*And goes off.*)

Mother (*turning pages*) I don't think she was very long working for us when that was taken. Cursed disease: whatever we did to deserve it.

Christy (*nods at another photograph*) Marie. Solemn.

Mother And she isn't like that at all! D'you know, Christy?! She's – practical – but of all of us, Marie is the one who lives in the present. She's the *easiest* of us all. D'you know, Christy?

Christy Yeh! – (*And points at another photograph:*) There's yourself.

Mother Yuk!

Christy (*laughing*) No! No!

Louise Oh! McCabe's are going to be fined for selling margarine as butter.

Mother Oh dear. (*The photograph of herself:*) Although I was trim. This diet and these damned pills that they have me on: (*She blows out her cheeks: diet/pills are bloating her.*)

Louise Well, see you!

Mother See you, love!

Louise 'Bye!

Mother Bye-bye, love!

Louise 'Bye!

Christy Louise!

Louise 'Bye!

She's gone. (In a moment, her car driving away.) **Mother** *turning more pages, stops at another photograph.*

Christy   Mr de Burca.

Mother   Yes. Jack. (*And she contains a sigh over the photograph of her husband and whatever happened to him.*)

Christy   The flowers he had here.

Mother (*correcting him*)   Wild flowers. He wouldn't let a plough or a scythe touch the Wide Ridge, that two-acre field up there. We spent all night out in it once. (*And now becomes a little embarrassed/shy.*) Before the, before the children were born of course, before – Wild flowers. And it all [life] should be so easy, Christy! (*She smiles at him.*) D'you know? And he loved this house.

Christy   Why d'you want to sell it then? (*Impetuously. And laughing in an attempt to be tactful in offering her assistance, financial, if that is the problem.*) D'you see what I mean?! Life is short, Mrs de Burca – isn't that what you're saying! Is it? And if it's a question of! D'you know what I mean? You may think it's none of my business but all the same, easy come, easy go is what I say! And if it's a question of the shillings, well! Because money means nothing! Oh-ho, absolutely, it's stupid! And I think there's very few people about that care! Mediocrity – it's scandalous! And who, therefore, should be short of a bob in this day and age?! It's easy come by – There's all sorts of ways of getting it – Making it – That is one fact – I know that! – And I don't care either! Mrs de Burca. I've a few bob, means nothing to me – And if it's a question of? . . . So, yeh see.

Mother   No, it's –

Christy   The wall is nearly done, Monday I put a bit of stuff on the drive – and anything else – whatever – and you're secure, all sorted out! What's wrong with that, where's the problem? Terrific! And if people'd be more happier staying put, live where they should be living, where they want to live, that is firmly what they should do – Stay put! Because, I mean to say, one good turn deserves another! Isn't that what they say? . . . D'you know what I'm saying? Mrs de Burca.

Mother   I do.

Christy   I hope you don't think I'm talking out of turn!

Mother   No. Thank you . . . It's not a question of the money.

Christy   Don't understand it then!

Mother   It's too big. Now. It isn't working out. And – Christy! – the past is the past.

Christy   Aw I don't know so much about that!

Mother   No –

Christy   You wouldn't change your mind?

Mother   No.

Christy   You might!

Mother   No.

Christy   Aw I don't know now!

Mother   And – Christy? No man about the place. Now, isn't it a pity that *Marie* and I are not good enough for you?

Christy   But, still, if you don't mind me saying so, you could be making a mistake.

Mother   (*smiles to herself that the import of her last is lost on him. Then:*)   Well, I suppose I could.

He nods to this, to himself.

Mother   (*finds another photograph*)   Who is this now? Who is that little boy?

Christy   (*merely glances at it*)   That's me. (*He isn't interested, he now has a bigger problem to consider.*) I think there was a bit of concrete left over that Peter mixed, and in case it goes hard, I'll just . . .

He goes off (to the wall). **Marie** *is coming from the house with a tray of lunch things, her eyes following him.*

Scene Five

The church bell for Mass. (It continues ringing.) Sunday morning.

Bunty*'s is dimly lit. (The blinds have not been let up, the door is shut.)*
Bunty *is cranky and uneasy, ushering* **Goldfish** *and* **Christy** *in the
back way.* **Goldfish** *has a pellet gun.*

Bunty   Jesus Christ, Jesus Christ. Sunday morning, wouldn't
you think it's up to Mass ye'd be going, be saying a few prayers
instead of breaking the licensing laws of God and man.

Goldfish   We was at Mass, man.

Bunty   I hope then ye heard Father Kilgarriff's sermon
about how to behave. What d'ye want, quick?

Christy   Martin?

Goldfish   Bottle of Time.

Christy *nods 'the same'.*

Bunty (*going off for drinks*)   What's the machine-gun for,
Goldfish?

Goldfish   That fuckin' bell. (*He has a headache.*)

Bunty (*returning with drinks*)   And if ye was at Mass, man, I
hope ye heard and heeded the prayer that's read out at all
Masses today.

Goldfish   We heard.

Bunty (*quoting*)   Guide all our emigrants down the right path
abroad, stop them from ever straying, teach them abstinence
and forbearance – did ye hear that? Keep them in mind of the
spiritual inheritance they took with them, the one true Church –

Goldfish   *What* did we take with us?

Bunty   And keep them in mind of the land of their birth so
that they may be fit one day to return to the bosom of thy
heavenly mansions yeh, amen. Did yeh hear that, Goldfish, did
yeh, when yeh was at Mass, man?

Goldfish   I did, Bunty.

Christy *gives him money for the drinks.*

Bunty (*going off*) Changing dollars for ye and whatnots.

Goldfish Fucker is making a fortune out of us. Yo-o!

They drink.

Fancy bit o' hunting? Better exercise than risking maybe balloonin' your bollix building a wall. (*Sips.*) Said I'd meet me bunch o' the guys 'bout one thirty up in the Square. Go on a shoot. Git us some prairie air, git us some wild turkey. (*Sips.*) Or one them thare buffaloes up in the hills. Git us a sheep?

Christy Pellets.

Goldfish Airgun, kid brother's. Still. (*Meaning, you could do damage with it.*) Take the eye out of a buff-sham?

Christy *laughs.*

Goldfish What – Hah – Chris – Yeh?! (*Celebration of the idea.*)

The church bell stops ringing: his acknowledgement of it:

Well, I do declare! Holy Joes: they hate us. But with cunning. We is varmint, man, outcasts, white trash. (*Sips.*) And I hate them.

Christy . . . How're yeh fixed?

Goldfish Dust? (*Gold-dust – money.*)

Christy (*nods*) I'm going to need a bit of money.

Goldfish Sure thing. Can drop you a ton?

Christy . . . Nah, it'll be all right.

The tapping of a coin on a plate-glass window from outside. And **Bunty** *is returning with change for* **Christy**. **Bunty**'s *reaction to the tapping and the following exchanges in whispers:*

Bunty Jesus Christ!

Peter (*off*) Bunty! (*More tapping.*)

Bunty Jesus Christ, Jesus Christ!

Jimmy (*off*)   Simon!

Bunty   Jesus Christ!

Peter (*off*)   Bunty, mate! (*More tapping.*)

Bunty   They can't wait twenty minutes for opening time.

Jimmy (*off*)   Simon! (*More tapping.*) Simon!

Bunty   They'll have the Church blackballing me. (*More tapping.*) Go round the back. (*More tapping.*) Go round the – friggin' back!

Peter (*off*)   Right, mate!

Jimmy (*off*)   Right, Simon!

Bunty (*going off*)   They'll cost me my licence.

Goldfish   And I hate farmers. Can't right figure out why. (*Sips.*) Yip, but I'm no son-o-fury if I don't come home sundown with a chicken.

Christy   . . . Still.

Goldfish   Chris?

Christy   All the same.

Goldfish   Yeh?

Christy   We come back every year.

Goldfish   That is a fact. And for what, I sure as shit don't know. Mother Macree?

Christy   Home.

Goldfish *looks at him.*
Home. (*Defensively.*)

Goldfish   Ho-ome?!

Christy   Yeh! Trees, landscape, air, fresh air.

Goldfish   Fresh air?

Christy   You said it yourself –

Goldfish   Landscape? –

Christy   Prairie air –

Goldfish   Trees?

Christy   Terrific – Yeh – They're perfect!

Goldfish   Firewood.

Bunty *is returning with* **Peter** *and* **Jimmy**, *the local.* **Peter** *in his petrol-blue mackintosh (as always),* **Jimmy** *in his Sunday suit and, for the record, there's nothing offensive in his behaviour today.*

Bunty   Ye're a disgrace to the country.

Goldfish   Pedro, Jaime!

Jimmy   Men!

Peter   Goldfish, Khrisht!

Goldfish   And how are we this fine day?

Bunty   Keep the voices down now – What d'ye want?

Jimmy   Pint please, Simon.

Bunty   You'll get no pint, I'm pouring no pints till half past twelve.

Jimmy   Bottle of Time please, Simon.

Peter   Yeh – And a small one too like, Bunt.

Bunty   And small one too like Bunt – (*His hand out to* **Peter** *for the money.* **Christy** *pays him.*) – and I'm dependent on the goodwill and permission of Church and State for my living. I'm surprised at you, Jimmy Toibin.

Jimmy   I was *at* Mass.

Bunty   You were at Mass, I know you were, with your mother, and now you're here! (*And he's gone.*)

Jimmy   What's up with *him*?

Goldfish   Bunty's eyes: The greed of the guy is [that's] already rich – Ever notice? (*Then, answering: 'what's up with him?'*)

Disturbed the man in his only pleasure in life: counting again last week's takings.

*They are amused. (Though the recurring references to **Bunty**'s revenue and wealth have begun to interest **Christy** privately. If he has to steal money, he will steal it.)*

Jimmy   As elegant as ever, Christy!

Peter   But the missus is up there now all right, in church like yeh know, with the mother and the kiddies. Saying her prayers with the best of them. She's English like, she's a convert. Oh, she converted all right and we was married in church and all, the other side. So who rightly should be watching me. Ay?

Bunty *returns with drinks and change.*

Jimmy   Thank you, Simon. (*To humour* **Bunty**:) Big dance tonight, boys?

Bunty   Did the priest call it out at whatever Mass you were at?

Jimmy   'Shamrock Ballroom, nine 'til three.' Oh, he does you the favour all right, Simon.

Bunty   And I do the favour for him. The church has to get their cut, haven't they?

Jimmy   For the Foreign Missions – he said that. – And that everyone should attend.

Goldfish   An' behave ourselves.

Bunty   He didn't mention the band? (*Hopeful that the priest did.*)

Jimmy   He didn't but doesn't everyone know! The Marveltones! And they don't sit down or anything! Only the drummer sits. And nearly all electric! Fancy steps forwards and back. And none of your black suits! Bright blue.

Goldfish   Get along!

Jimmy   Aw jays, the Marveltones.

Peter   Yeh like?!

Jimmy A mighty orchestra.

Bunty And a mighty price I have to guarantee them even if no one comes. Ye'll all be there, will ye?

Jimmy Oh, we'll be there, spot the talent.

Goldfish Charvering stakes'll be good with the girls, Simon?

Bunty (*admonishes him with his finger*) With the 'tache on yeh!

Goldfish Okay, gonna plassie me up nice lollylickin' tender fat boy then.

Bunty I provide ye with drink, dancing and the pictures and this's the thanks for the risks I take. (*And he's gone again.*)

Jimmy Luck, men, Christy!

Peter God bless!

Goldfish Fucker is a millionaire. Yo-o!

They drink, ritualistically.

Peter (*smiling*) But a strange thing. I wakes up this morning. Was it early? Was and all, mate, was and all. And I'm lying there like I'm drowning. Like it happens [at] times, the other side, but does you expect it at home – ay? But my eyes is so open, like you'd see in a man doesn't want to cry. You've a problem here, Peter. And the missus is there, asleep like. Kiddies over there. Snore from the mother [in] the next room. Well, this's a good one: What is it you have to do, Peter? Up I gets, puts on the togs. I'll go down the town for a gloak at the Square. Not much stirring, was there? Not half. And I'm stood in John P. Hogan's archway. Not much stirring. Dog across, asleep in O'Grady's doorway like. Nice bit of a setter in him. And I starts the walking. I mean I does the streets, I'm walking. And: Well, this's a quare thing: You're getting no satisfaction out of all this walking, Peter. Back to John P.'s archway. Then, whatever time it was, six, seven, bit of a stir. They're answering the bell. People like. Not that many mind, 'cause 'twas that very early Mass. But, you might as well, I says: Do the business. Up I goes, goes in and all, to the church like, and I says my own few prayers. And that's me kitted out for the

week. Back to the Square. John P.'s archway. Stood there. Dog
across, beginning to scratch the neck, stretch the back legs like.
And I starts the walking *again* – Ay? Till I remember: What did
I tell you before? You're only exerting yourself, Peter: Aren't
you on your holidays? Back to – (*Thumbs it: John P. Hogan's
archway.*) A good one – Ay? Till Jimmy here come along ten
minutes ago ... Ay? And I do –

Goldfish (*quietly, on a sigh*)   Haaaay, Pedro man, you is
talking Peruvian again.

Peter (*laughing*)   Am I, am I talking Peruvian again, Goldfish?

Goldfish   Fucker won't give us another 'til twelve thirty.

Jimmy   It's nearly that anyhow. I'll try him in a minute.

Peter   And I do dream about it: Coming home and all.

Goldfish   Where's yo' bin? – Ah's bin in bed with mah
honey, where's yo' bin?

Bit of a laugh – **Jimmy** *and* **Peter**.

Jimmy   Ah's bin in bed with mah honey!

Bunty (*off*)   Keep the voices down!

Jimmy   ... You're quiet, Christy.

Peter   Something must have worn him out last night ... And
the old nerves is going in the mother. Aw she's gone very bad
with them. And I gives her seventy quid and all for herself. But
it's coming up about the wedding photo I sent home four years
ago. Me and the missus like, was stood outside St Chad's in
Brum. She's questioning it. No, ma'am, I says, I don't know
who'd be putting that in your head: That who'd be saying the
arch around us in the photo isn't real at all, isn't the arch
around the doorway of St Chad's, but was only took in a
studio. You know how they can do it in a studio?

*Christy makes some movement, straightens up as a man might to adjust
his belt.*

Peter   Ay? (*To* **Christy**.)

Jimmy *misinterprets – touches* **Christy**'s *shoulder – thinks* **Christy** *is getting out his money for the next round, and reasonably, generously:*

Jimmy   Hold your horses there, Christy, you got the last one: let me –

And it's very sudden and very violent (though not very loud): **Christy** *has* **Jimmy** *by the face, has him swept back against the wall – a stool is knocked over? – and is banging the back of* **Jimmy**'s *head against the wall.*

Bunty (*off*)   Noise!

Goldfish   'S okay, man!

Christy   Know what I mean, Jimmy?

Jimmy   Jesus, what's this –? (*All about.*)

Christy   Na-na-na, know what I mean? (*Banging* **Jimmy**'s *head.*)

Bunty (*off*)   Noise!

Goldfish   Right, Simon, 's okay, Simon, everythin's under control!

Jimmy   For fuck's –

Christy   Na-na-na-na-na! Jimmy? Where d'*you* belong? I'd kill for here! Would you kill for here? I'd kill! Know what I mean? Know-what-I-mean?!

Jimmy   I don't! I don't, Christy!

Christy   . . . No provoke.

And he releases him. **Jimmy** *is practically in tears.* **Christy** *is trembling.* **Goldfish** *is delighted, beats a silent drum roll, and* sotte voce:

Goldfish   Hee-haw! (*Then:*) Hey, you guys, take it easy! Pedro, you were saying!

Peter   Ay?

Goldfish   Weddin' photo, man: proceed.

Peter   No, ma'am, I'm saying, to the mother like, Goldfish, that's not a studio, that's St Chad's.

Goldfish   And she's (*saying*) – Huh? – Registry Office. I dig, kid.

Peter   She's (*saying*) – D'yeh dig, Goldfish? And is the kiddies, was they even ever like baptised?

Goldfish   Well, I'll be!

Peter   Nerves is going in her.

Bunty (*returning, relaxed now, looking at his pocket watch*)   And as you did not forget St Joseph, the Blessed Virgin and the Baby Jesus on their flight into Egypt, remember now we humbly beseech thee our emigrants abroad – What was that rumpus about?

He has continued off, to let up his blinds, open his front door. Daylight coming into the bar. And the church bell is ringing again, the end of Mass.

Goldfish (*to* **Peter**)   Yup?

Peter   And was my missus, is my missus the landlady I took up with. Naaw, naaw, ma'am, I keeps saying: My missus ain't no landlady, naaw, and tell that to whoever's putting it in your head. I wouldn't marry, Goldfish – I ain't never rode a landlady the other side. She's a woman, ma'am, I keeps telling her, like everyone else, a convert. Ay?

Bunty (*returning – and continues off again*)   So that they may be fit one day to return to the bosom of thy heavenly mansions yeh, amen.

Goldfish (*calling after him*)   Two bottles Time – Simon! – drop of whiskey for Pedro –

Christy   Not for me –

Goldfish   And Jimmy-kid's pint! (*To* **Christy**:) Ay?

Christy   Have to go.

Goldfish   Don't fancy bit big-game huntin' then? *You* can have the gun.

Christy Y'haven't something smaller – a Luger? See you in here tonight. (*Calls:*) Simon! (*And thumbs-up sign:*) See you later. (*Tap on the shoulder to* **Peter**, *another to* **Jimmy**, *and he's gone.*)

Peter Ta-ta, Khrisht!

The church bell stops ringing.

Goldfish Well, I do declare, that wasn't such a bad little Mass after all! You fixin' that round – Simon! – yes or what, minus one Time?

Bunty (*off*) Yes!

Goldfish And, with the good Lord's help, they'll be better little one to come! But what d'yeh pray for?

Peter Ay?

Goldfish 'So up I goes an' all like', you said – To church – 'an' I says my own few prayers.'

Peter Like?

Goldfish What d'yeh pray for?

Peter For? . . . Some of God's grace like . . . So that I'd understand.

Goldfish Understand? Understand what?

Peter I don't know like.

Goldfish *continues to look at him, his sincerity.*

Jimmy (*to no one*) Jesus Christ! (*Reaction to the experience he has had.*)

Goldfish (*to himself*) Jesus Christ.

Scene Six

Dining room. De Burcas'. Six chairs around a table set for Sunday lunch. (This room is part of a double room. Note: The house is a four/five-bedroom affair, early Victorian.) **Mother** *and* **Louise** *are standing by, waiting. Sunday clothes.* **Mother** *has a glass of sherry.* **Louise** *is* *wearing a hat with a half-veil and she will sit to lunch in it. (She has a black eye.) And she's wearing her 'new' earrings.*

Mother   No Michael?

Louise   He had to go to – oh some GAA thing, a match.

Mother   . . . Very nice. (*Admiring the table.*)

Marie (*coming in with a tureen of soup, calling*)   Susanne!

Mother   Spoiled. (*She sits.*)

Marie   Michael isn't coming?

Louise *shakes her head and sits.*

Marie   So we won't need this one. (*She removes a chair.*) Susanne!

Susanne (*off*)   Coming!

Marie (*serving soup*)   Isn't Sheila Kerrigan looking well!

Mother   Isn't she looking well! Thank you, love, thank you. I'm spoiled . . . Were you talking to Sheila, Louise?

Louise *shakes her head.*

Marie   And the new baby, did you see it?

Mother   Beautiful!

Marie   Susanne!

Susanne   Anseo! (*'Present'*)

She has made an entrance in an elegant dress (more suited to evening wear, perhaps); her hair arranged up. To **Mother**'s *chair to kiss the top of* **Mother**'s *head. Then:*

Now, what can I do to help?

Marie   Sit down! (*And laughs.*)

Susanne   Oh, the hat! (**Louise**'s)

Marie   The dress!

(*Note: The vacant fifth chair is Father's: a mark of* **Mother**'s *ongoing love for her late husband.*)

Susanne Nice Mass?

Mother Yes!

Marie They do go on though with their announcements. And that prayer for emigrants? (*Questioning its taste.*)

Mother (*agrees*) I thought that. Feeling better, love, headache gone?

Susanne Yes, thank you.

Marie Oh! (*She has forgotten something and is up again, leaving the room hastily.*)

Susanne 'Gallop apace, you fiery-footed steed towards Phoebus' lodging!'

Marie (*off*) 'Such a waggoner as Phaeton would whip you to the west!'

Mother (*not performing / chuckling*) 'And bring in cloudy night im*med*iately! Spread thy close curtain, love-performing night.' Is it? Susanne? 'That runaway's-eyes may wink. And Romeo leap to these arms . . .' Mmmm! (*The soup.*)

Susanne Leeep! 'To these arms untalked of and unseen.'

Louise Is that a new dress?

Susanne This old thing? – Yes . . . D'you like it?

Louise Mm. Where'd you buy it?

Susanne A present . . . Do you like it, Mother?

Mother Absolutely – Mm soup, Marie!

Marie (*returning with a bottle of wine*) 'Come, gentle night; come, loving black-browed night, give me my Romeo; and when he shall die, take him and cut him out in little stars, and he will make the face of heaven so fine, that all the world will be in love with night and pay no worship . . . to the garish sun' – Oh dear! (*She laughs, suddenly self-conscious, as if she had betrayed a secret. Then:*) Wine!

Mother   Why not!

Susanne   It's not as if it's exactly winter. (*They don't know what she is talking about.*) And I'm out in – the dew – in it. This dress.

Mother   Love?

Susanne   Only sensitive people with poetic minds catch TB.

Marie, *pouring wine, laughs at her sister's personality.*

Susanne   Thank you. (*For wine.*) Anyway, I don't much like it myself. (*Her dress.*)

Mother (*very informal raising of her glass*)   It's so seldom we're all together any more. (*Sips. Grins.*) Or-that-we'll-be-here much *longer.*

Marie   We'll be fine. Well, good luck everybody!

They drink.

Louise   And did you see the size of Catherine Healy?

Marie   Is she pregnant, Louise?

Louise (*remembers that she is wretched*) *shakes her head, she doesn't know.*

Susanne   It could be all that fresh white bread you have started to eat around here.

Marie *frowning, to work out* **Susanne***'s remark, then she laughs.*

Mother   Though – and I don't know that it's too much to ask – why a woman like me, or a half-woman like me –

Marie   Mum! –

Mother   With three healthy – beautiful! – daughters shouldn't want a grandchild.

They laugh – or appropriate individual reactions.

What is wrong with my girls?

They laugh.

Marie   You can rent one, Mum. We'll be fine.

Susanne   ... What happens to the table?

Mother   Love?

Susanne   This. (*Table.*) Has it been considered? The auction happens on – Tuesday? Does it?

Mother   Yes, it –

Susanne   And for instance – I know it for a fact – the sideboard is worth a hundred pounds.

Mother   As much as that, how interesting.

Susanne   Well, Louise can hardly have use for it in a run-down pub, and even if it fitted above the shop for you and Marie, I do not see how anyone, possibly, could get it up those narrow stairs. The furniture. This is what we should be discussing instead of – hiver-hovering.

Marie   Hiver?! (*And laughs.*)

Mother   And are you sure – Susanne – that that's where I should go? That I should move in over the shop with Marie.

Susanne   I am merely pointing out, Mum!

Mother   And are you sure that Marie should have an old woman move in over the shop with her?

Marie   Mum.

Mother   Should you?

Marie   Yes. We'll be fine. Now – children, children – eat up, drink your soup!

Susanne (*to herself*)   God's sake! ... I am merely – (*She stops herself with a sigh.*) ... But I find I am becoming very frustrated.

Mother   Oh dear. When it's sold and our obligations are met you will all get your share.

Susanne *is hurt/angered – both – by this.*

Marie   ... Isn't the wall looking – terrific?

Mother   Those boys (*She pushes out her glass for a top-up.*)

Marie? And when they leave again, as they'll be leaving, soon, and Christy, I wonder what kind of life, what kind of reception, have they to go back to.

Susanne (*to herself*) I could tell you a few things about that.

Mother Thank you, love. (*To* **Marie** *for the top-up.*)

Marie Susanne? ('*More wine?*')

Susanne I couldn't care less about 'my share'! That is not what I am talking about, that is not the point!

Mother And what is the point?

Susanne Oh, this has become an absurd conversation!

Marie Why continue with it then? More wine?

Susanne No, thank you ... The point is I am never consulted about anything in this family.

Mother What did we not consult you about? Selling the table?

Susanne Cheap! Selling the whole place, for instance.

Mother You were consulted –

Susanne I wasn't.

Mother I write to you regularly –

Susanne Oh, writing letters, yes –

Mother But you don't appear to read what I write.

Susanne Letters about her (*Louise.*) and Michael Burgess's drinking problems – perhaps that is the real reason why the place is being sold: to rescue the run-down hole of a business she married into. And that will be more money down the drain – literally! Letters about – the dog! Letters about Marie and her problems – Everybody's problems!

Marie What problems?

Louise Don't address me as –

Susanne I get depressed too, I get lonely too, I am not

made of steel, I should like to be treated with respect, I am part
of this family too – I hope – but I find I am becoming very left
out.

Louise Don't –

Marie *What* is your problem, Susanne?

Louise Marie, I wish you'd let me speak –

Susanne Would this place be – sacrificed – for me if I were
– distressed? Hah!

Louise Susanne, don't address me as 'she'.

Mother And are you?

Susanne What?

Mother Distressed?

Susanne I'm not.

Marie More soup for anyone or has everyone finished?

Mother We are selling – I wrote to you about it – because
we are under *some* financial pressure and because, now –

Susanne You won't get me to agree, Mother!

Mother (*to* **Louise**) D'you have a cigarette?

Louise *has no cigarettes.*

Susanne … But if any one of you thinks that I'll be back
again to stay in somebody's *box*room over somebody's shop or
pub, you are all making a great mistake.

Marie (*to herself*) Impossible.

Susanne If that matters, of course.

Mother Are you saying we *shouldn't* sell?

Susanne I didn't say that.

Mother Then you're saying that we should.

Susanne I'm saying – I'm saying –

Marie Your bowl, Susanne –

Susanne I'm saying – I'm saying, even if I'm away, I belong here. I'd like to have some – standing! Somewhere! I'm saying, I'm saying . . . (*She has become very emotional. Perhaps she is crying.*) Standing! What else is there? . . . Mum . . . Mum . . . I'm saying . . .

Mother (*to herself, silently – a sigh?*) Oh dear. (*Then, gently:*) I know, love.

Susanne Had I been consulted, *properly*, I could have come up with alternatives.

Marie And your alternatives?

Mother Love? (*To* **Susanne**.)

Susanne I said I *could* have, I *could* have!

Marie (*to herself, again*) Impossible. SOUP BOWLS!

They begin to comply with their soup bowls.

Susanne Could I have a glass of wine, please? . . . And there is little or no interest in the place as far as I can see so it is going to go for a song. To some – dolt – no doubt. And you are not concerned. Thank you. (*For the wine.*) And you think that I too should stand idly by? Well, we shall see about that, oh yes we shall. At the auction, I shall be standing here –

Marie Oh, come along!

Susanne And you make me laugh! (*An extremely rude snap. Rises.*) Oh, give the place away, I don't care, let it all fall down. (*To* **Louise**.) Are the earrings new?

Louise 'A present!'

Mother Then let it! Fall down. Susanne!

Susanne *gestures that she has risen to assist with the crockery.*

Mother*'s anger is untypical. (But* **Susanne** *has the capacity to test people to their limit: a self-destructive drive that will find its final accommodation yet.)* **Mother** *is ill, she's a widow, she is worried about her three daughters and their futures, there is 'some' financial pressure on* *her, and coming to a decision to sell the family home has been difficult and complex. She keeps trying to contain her outburst, and failing – even to her final 'I'm sorry'.*

Mother   The strain, worry, effort it has been, to stop everything from falling down! To carry on! To keep it all standing! ... Since your father was *taken* from me! ... If any one of you had had an alternative plan for here, well then! We would have managed it, somehow! If that would have settled you! ... That would have been a different matter! ... Life disappearing – How much can one take?! ... And though we are selling, this house is not 'a place', and I will not have it referred to as such around your father's table! It was his dream! And mine! ... It was our home, once: Now it's not ... I'm sorry!

All of them are upset. **Mother** *regrets her outburst, head turning to the vacant fifth chair, to sigh, or contain it, propping her jaw with her fist.* **Susanne** *feels remorse but she cannot help herself and, in a moment, she will walk out, the offended party, bridling herself.* **Louise** *touches her eyes under her veil.* **Marie**'s *characteristic frown; now she abandons her dishes to follow* **Susanne** *out of the room to have a word with her.*

Lights down for a passage of time. Dance-hall music, faint, wafted on a breeze from the town. Sunday night.

Marie, *frozen in time, is looking out at the gathering night and at whatever else might be out there.* **Mother**, *with a glass of port and a cigarette, is seated.* **Louise**, *head bowed, is weeping quietly, seated beside* **Mother**. *Her hat and veil are on the table. She has a black eye.*

Mother   Louise? Love? ... Louise? Love?

Louise   What?

Mother   What you're doing is ... foolish. (*'Foolish', a more diplomatic word than her first choice, 'childish'*) ... Louise?

Louise   What?

Mother   I'm sorry. I shouldn't have let you marry him. I should have ... somehow ... stopped you ... But you are married to him. There are rules ... Louise? Love?

Marie (*comes out of her reverie*)   I might have something out
here. (*She goes out.*)

Mother   Love? Is it sore? . . . Marie will find something to
put on it . . . Love? I understand people's needs. I amn't
criticising you. But . . . (*She smiles to herself; she doesn't have the
words.*) It's a dream. A mystery, a nightmare. (*Decides against the
last.*) A dream . . . Love, what you're doing is wrong. And it
isn't doing you any good. What you're doing is only making
you unhappy. Love?

Louise *shakes her head.*

Mother   You're not being fair to yourself. Or to *others* . . . It's
not the answer . . . You know who and what I mean . . . Love?

Louise (*a whisper*)   I hate him!

*There is ambivalence in the 'him', but as she rises she pulls off her 'new'
earrings.*

Mother   Love?

Louise   Then the answer is, I shall go away too.

Mother (*as to a child*)   Oh!

Louise (*collects her hat*)   Mum. (*Kisses her.*)

Mother   Would you like to stay?

Louise *shakes her head.* **Marie** *has returned with some cotton wool
and a bottle. She treats* **Louise**'s *eye.*

Marie   This will help for a bit now.

Louise   It's okay, I'm okay, it's fine, I'm fine – Marie!

Marie   Shhhhh! Come over to the shop to me in the
morning.

Louise   Goodnight.

Mother   Goodnight, love.

Marie (*going out with* **Louise**)   I'll sell you a nice pair of
sunglasses?

Mother (*alone*)   Oh dear! (*Part laugh-sigh-sob.*)

Marie   (*off*)   Goodnight! Drive carefully!

Louise's *car driving off.* **Marie** *returns to her place at the window, to look out.*

Marie (*to herself, absently*)   Oh dear! (*She remembers* **Mother**.) Hm?

Mother   'Oh dear!' (*They share a smile.*)

Marie   Is *she* going to emigrate too?

Mother   And from what we see of it, this emigration, whether from necessity or discontent, isn't doing much good for anyone.

Marie   Tired?

Mother   No. Why don't you put on that other dress and go up to that dance-thing for an hour or two. I'm fine.

Marie   No. (*She switches on the radio: Gigli singing 'I'll walk beside you' – or some instrumental piece.*)

Mother   And Oh – dear – Susanne! (*Clenched fist; grinning.*)

Marie's *humouring laugh.*

Mother   I don't understand her, I never did! . . . And 'hiver-hovering'?!

Marie   Yes!

Mother   Where does she learn that – language? . . . She hasn't gone, she didn't take her suitcase?

Marie   No.

Mother   Will she come home tonight?

Marie (*doesn't know.*)   She said, 'I am going up town for a breath of fresh air.' (*And laughs again to make things right.*)

Mother   I shouldn't have spoken out like that.

Marie   Oh, I don't know.

Mother (*to herself*)   Mistakes.

Marie   Mistakes? Everyone does the best they can. There should be, and maybe there could be, an ideal world, but there isn't.

Mother   And she drives too fast.

Marie   I've just been philosophising and you weren't even listening.

Mother (*smiles. But in the next moment, to herself:*)   But I get the *strangest* notions. D'you know. ('*Strangest*': *foreboding.*)

Marie   That's lovely, isn't it? (*The song/music on the radio.*)

Mother   . . . Does she have a boyfriend?

Marie   Yes, but it's a secret: *he* doesn't know it yet.

Mother   Not the actor one she brought home a few years ago?

Marie   No.

Mother   I didn't like him.

Marie   This one owns a nightclub, my dear – or several of them.

Mother   Well, God help him whoever gets her . . . And do you?

Marie   Hm?

Mother   Have a secret man.

Marie (*smiles. Then:*)   I'm awaiting him.

Mother   *Did* I consult you properly about selling?

Marie   You have the lot of us on the roadside! You did. We'll be fine.

Mother (*nods*)   . . . Marie: Louise, in what she does, is immature; and Susanne is a snob. Now, I am not a snob and neither was your father: and if there were someone – secret man – all three of us could live together in one little house. If *you* made the move.

Marie   Mmmm!

Mother   Because, in certain matters, men aren't . . . so bright. D'you know?

Marie *nods solemnly.*

Mother   And, because life *is* short. D'you know?

Marie   Mmmm!

Mother   Love?

Marie   Well, d'you know what I think? This may surprise you. D'you know what I'm going to tell you? I think, Mum, you've begun to hiver-hover.

Mother *starts to chuckle.*

Marie   Come on, bed, you're exhausted. (*Taking* **Mother***'s glass, extinguishing the cigarette:*) And you have enough of these. (*To the radio, humming whatever song/tune is now playing, to switch it off.*)

Mother (*addressing herself, rising*)   You're a foolish, wicked, bad old woman.

Dance-hall music, faint, from the distance. **Marie** *escorting* **Mother** *off; they go off.* **Marie** *returns to switch off the lights. On her way out again, she stands in the window, moonlit, to look out.*

Marie   Come, gentle night.

Scene Seven

Bunty*'s bar is crowded (as can be).* **Bunty** *is in and out, serving his two bars.* **Christy** *(in shirt-sleeves) is playing volunteer pot-boy. People at the counter have their hands raised for drink, including* **Jimmy** *(who, this evening, is on his own — or in company other than* **Peter** *–* **Goldfish** *–* **Christy***.)*

Jimmy   Simon! Simon! –

Tarpey *is present, in civvies. He wears a hat at an angle. He is a* *small-town figure of authority. He knows it. He's perhaps fifty. (We saw him at the top of Scene Two.) He's waiting for someone.*

The dance hall is across the street. The music is loud. A quickstep. (Slow dances will be quiet.) One can see, but it's hard to hear, what people are saying.

Bunty (*taking a drink to* **Tarpey**)   You're all right here, Inspector, are you? Now, this is on me. You'll go across, will you, to the dance for a few minutes? Now, a pass for you. ('*A pass*', *a complimentary card/ticket.*)

Jimmy   Simon! –

Bunty   In a minute! (*As he goes out to his other bar.*)

Peter *and* **Goldfish** *are together.* **Goldfish** *is impatient, he wants to go to the dance, now.* **Peter** *is literally twisted with drink.*

Peter   Bunty! Mate!

Goldfish   No!

Peter   We'll have one more.

Goldfish   You've *got* the hooch! In your pocket, man! Chris!

The last, a call to say that they are leaving, to **Christy** *who is taking a crate of empties out the back.*

Christy   See you across in a while! (*And he's gone.*)

Goldfish   Mosey, Pedro, let's breeze, man!

Jimmy   (*from his place*)   A round in here, Simon!

Peter   Khrisht! (*Announcing that they're leaving, though* **Christy** *is well gone.*)

Goldfish   Go-go-go-go-go! (*He's gone.*)

Peter   (*his glass drained*)   Wait for me, Goldfish! (*He's gone.*)

Susanne *has entered the scene, looking for diversion.*

Jimmy   Simon!

Bunty   (*Returning*)   Yes, Jimmy?

Christy *is returning with a crate of beer for* **Bunty**.

Bunty   Thanks, Christy!

There is not much in here up to **Susanne**'s *mark and she is leaving again.*

Christy   Susanne! Susanne!

Susanne   . . . Me?

Christy   Going across?

Susanne   Sorry?

Christy (*joining her*)   Are you going to the dance?

Bandleader (*off; muffled*)   Thank you, boys and girls, next dance, please.

A lull in the music.

Christy   Were you across there already?

Susanne   I had a peep.

Christy   Are you going back over there again?

Susanne   Mmmm. (*Keeping her options open.*)

Christy   Fancy something?

Susanne   I might go home. G and T.

Christy   Gin and tonic, Simon!

Bunty (*calling a greeting*)   Susanne, isn't it? (*He's busy with* **Jimmy**/*someone.*)

Susanne   I think so!

Christy   Classy dress.

Susanne   This place is only fit for troglodytes.

He laughs. (He's eager about something.)

And how are we this evening?

Christy   Top of the world!

Susanne   When do you go back to London?

Christy   Well now, that is an interesting question. I don't know that I'll be going back. (*He grins.*)

Bunty (*calling*)   Enjoying the holidays?

Susanne   Right!

Christy   The auction happens Tuesday.

Susanne   Does it? Are you working here?

Christy   Nah. Just giving him a hand.

Susanne   Hmm? (*She's checking the place for a better prospect than* **Christy***'s company.*)

Christy   Actually, I'm glad I ran into you because there's a matter that was bothering me. You won't believe this, but I thought that if I could see *you*. Because I wouldn't mind having a chat. Yeh know?

Susanne   With me?

Christy   Yeh. I can't discuss it with Mrs de Burca, not yet. That wouldn't be fair. Terrific woman. Yeh know? Her kindness. Treated me like a son almost.

Susanne (*glancing about again*)   Yeh, she's like that.

Christy   I sound stupid.

Susanne   But you have lovely hands.

Christy   Them.

Susanne   Dem hands. What do you do on the building sites to have lovely things like those?

Christy   Oh! Gloves.

Susanne   Do you? They wear gloves now and everything on the building sites?

Bunty   Now, Susanne, gin and tonic, welcome home! Thanks, Christy son! (*Money. And is gone out to his other bar.*) Yeh.

Christy   It's hard to talk here. Would you like to take these [drinks] outside, or? Hm?

Susanne   Fast mover. This will do fine. You would like to discuss in private your intimate thoughts with me: I understand, how well I understand! (*She is laughing knowingly.*)

Christy   No! No! (*Laughing.*)

Susanne   And you cannot have a *chat* with *Louise*?

Christy ('*No*'.)   But we could always talk, you and me – Remember?

Susanne   Or Marie?

Christy   Marie? ('*Hardly.*') But this matter that's been bothering me all week: well, I've come to a decision about it.

Susanne   No, tell me first – No, tell me about Louise first! What is going on between the builder's labourer and that child?

Christy   Nothing.

Susanne   Nothing? Aaa! You can tell me – if we could always talk.

Bandleader (*off*)   And the next dance, boys and girls, will be a slow waltz. (*Music, muted.*)

Christy   Okay. There was – (*Shrugs – 'some little thing'.*) It's over.

Susanne   Aaa! You can give me the details. What do you do to her?

Christy   Okay. Louise came to me one night. Story about your man, Burgess.

Susanne   Her husband, right?

Christy   I never liked him. How he was treating her. The town's great all-round athlete one time: look at him now. I had a word with him. Gave him a few slaps, didn't I? I was glad – Yeh. Frankly – that she came to me. And . . . It

became a bit involved. But hands off that now. Louise is
perfect – in many ways – but she's a married woman.

Susanne   . . . I think you would possess us all.

Christy What?

Susanne And how far have you got with Marie?

Christy Marie?

Susanne The one with her head screwed on, and who is
– she told me herself – three years and one month, exactly
to the day, older than you: What naughty things have you
been doing to our Marie?

Christy (*smiles/whatever at the very idea of this. Then:*) Yeh, I
suppose it's only natural Marie disapproves of me.

Susanne Really?

Christy Has always done.

Susanne Is that a fact now?

Christy What? And, at the same time, there's times . . .

Susanne When you think what?

Christy That maybe I'm getting it wrong.

Susanne *winks to herself in the broad, shrewd manner.*

Christy Because, there's times when I think, it's maybe
that she's . . .

Susanne Perfect.

Christy Yeh. Dead straight.

Susanne And it's been killing her for years. (*They laugh?*)
But you've turned the heads of the lot of them! Except me.

Christy But, you and me, we used to share some secrets
down that place of yours one time. D'you not remember?

Susanne Oh, it's the *past* you want to chat about?

Christy 'The Princess!' (*He bows to her.*) I had to tell all my secrets to the princess. D'you not –

Susanne I do not remember. I deal in reality. The past
is a pig. Anyway, Marie was the princess – the queen! –
the king! That's Marie again you're thinking about. *She*
demanded the tributes – and *got* them! Flowers, prizes,
secrets – Consultations, when they happened, were – are! –
always with her! Your vows of unending love. She took you
very seriously. Still does! The sensible one. She dressed you
up, for God's sake! In frillies! (*He's laughing.*) Ah, but do you
see, kinky stuff, what? Yeah?!

Christy Well, I've a secret for you now. This's going to
surprise you. And the reason why I tell you is: I wouldn't
like to think that anything I do'd come as such a surprise –
shock even – specially to Mrs de Burca. Eternally fond of
her, eternally grateful. Well, that place of yours down there:

Susanne It's not 'a place.'

Christy No. Heaven on earth. I'm going to buy it . . .

Susanne *starts laughing at him.*

Christy It's going to surprise people all right.

Susanne (*laughing*) This is some chat-up line!

Christy I'm serious.

Susanne (*still laughing – in a silly way*) Don't be so fucking
stupid! (*Still laughing.*) Tell me, how far have you got with
Mrs de Burca?

Kerrigan *comes in. When he's drunk he's loud – he shouts – and
most everything is on a laugh. He's drunk.*

Kerrigan Time, gentlemen, please! Can't ye see the Law
is there?! (**Tarpey.**) I'm late, Inspector! And what harm
itself if I am! Have ye no homes to go to?! Ah, the
peasantry! 'Have we not seen, round Britain's peopled
shore,/Our useful sons exchanged for useless ore?!' Why
aren't ye across there, hoppin' an' leppin' like sensible
people for the poor aul Black Babies in Africa?! Oh be the
hokies, Miss de Burca! Sweet Auburn, loveliest village lassie

of the plain! And you never got married? Look at that
now, a fine-looking woman like you! And you must have
had great chances! What're yeh talking to this fella for? –
The hero, Valentino. Come on, dance for your daddy!
Law-law-law-law, lal-lal-lal-lal-lal-lal, lal-lal-lal-law . . . !

He has danced her away from **Christy**. **Susanne** *protesting the
attention she is getting. He is dancing her to where* **Tarpey** *is
drinking:*

I'm late, Inspector, but can't you see I've better things to
be doing?! Law-law law-law. . . ! Sure you know this/that
handsome man here/there! (*Introducing them:*) Richard Tarpey
of Ireland's finest: Miss Susan de Burca!

Susanne   Susanne!

Kerrigan   Susanne! De Burca de [the] Hon! Innkeeper! –
where is he? Bunty! Drinks in here!

Susanne   Are you going to the dance? (*To* **Tarpey**.)

Kerrigan   He's *not* going to the dance, *I'm* going to the
dance! Ah, 'Sweet Auburn, loveliest village of the plain/
where health and plenty cheer the labouring swain . . .' (*etc.,
as required: 'The Deserted Village', Goldsmith.*)

Goldfish *exasperated, has come in, joined* **Christy**. *And, in a
moment,* **Peter**.

Goldfish (*calls*)   Small one there!

Christy   What's doin'?

Goldfish (*sighs*)   'Jerry, please help me.' (*Bette Davis, though
he is not amused.*)

Peter   Wouldn't let us in, Khrisht.

Goldfish   They wouldn't let *him* in. Then, when I got
involved – Jesus!

Peter   Pack of fuckers.

Christy   'Shall ve just have a cigarette on it?' (*Paul Henreid
– 'Now Voyager.' Though* **Christy** *isn't amused either at this
stage.*)

Goldfish Small one, Simon.

Bunty (*coming in*) I heard yeh!

Peter Your missus in the box office wouldn't let us into the dance, Bunty.

Bunty No more drink in here for him tonight.

Goldfish Am *I* getting a drink?

Bunty In a minute, wait your turn! Now, Inspector, ye want something over here?

Kerrigan Whiskey! In a dirty glass. And another of whatever he's having! And, Miss Susanne?

Bunty Gin and tonic.

Susanne Oh, all right.

Kerrigan 'The bashful virgin's side-long looks of love,/ The matron's glance that would those looks reprove!'

Bunty *has gone off again for* **Kerrigan***'s round.*

Peter And look! (*A fistful of paper money.*)

Goldfish Easy there.

Peter And look!

Goldfish Put it away – Sit down – Sit! Can't you see lawyers, attorneys is present, an' ladies an' lawmen? *More* ladies.

'More ladies' refers to **Louise** *who has come in. (Hair arranged over her injured eye.)*

Kerrigan Where's-your-husband?!

Louise Where's your wife? (*And joins the party.*)

Bunty *is returning with* **Kerrigan***'s round:*

Bunty Last orders!

Kerrigan 'The curfew tolls the knell of parting day!'

Susanne 'The lowing herd winds slowly o'er the lea/The ploughman homeward plods his weary way/And leaves the world to darkness –'

Kerrigan 'And to dust –'

Susànne 'And to *me*'! –

Kerrigan Dust! –

Susanne Me! –

Bunty (*before going out again*)   Throw this out the back for me, Christy.

Christy *goes out with another crate of empties.*

Bandleader (*off*)   Thank you, boys and girls, next dance, please.

Bunty (*off*)   Last orders!

Goldfish Small whiskey? (*Casually to nobody, and sighs.*)

Kerrigan These British Tommies, these British soldiers – Susanne! – gunners, are in the dug-out, waiting for the German planes to come –

Susanne Fokkers! – I heard it! –

Kerrigan No, you didn't hear this one! But, anyway – Susanne! – the British officer in charge has a stammer and he warns them: 'W-wait 'til I give the s-signal to f-fire.' Now the German planes are coming, now the German planes are in the gunners' sights, now they're in range, and the officer goes: 'F-f-f-f-f-f-f – Fuck them, we'll get them on the way back.'

Hilarity.

Peter Pack of fuckers! (*To himself.*)

He's a man in and out of a stupor. He has discovered the bottle of drink (mentioned at the top of the scene) in his pocket. He's really talking about the people outside. But he hardly knows where he is. He's lost, impotent, enraged. He offers a drink to **Goldfish**. **Goldfish** *shakes his head.*

Peter   The poxy pack of fuckers in this town. Watching me. Talking about me.

Goldfish   Take it easy, amigo.

Peter   Ay? Ay? . . . Well, if anyone'd raise, raise a, raise one – (*finger*) – to my, to one of my, my children, the kiddies like, to my missus, I'd . . . Or say a, or say one – boo – to them, about them, I'd . . . I'd!

Goldfish   Easy, can't you? Quality is present, man.

Peter   Or to me, mate.

Goldfish   Relax, can't you, like me?

Peter   Ain't? Ain't? That I, that I, that I ain't a Catholic, is it? Ay? That I, that my missus, my children, the kiddies, ain't? Ain't baptised?! . . . Are! Fuckin' are and all, mate!

Goldfish   Hey, man, Pedro –

Peter   Well, would they like now, this minute like, like to say it to me now like? To my fuckin' face like, like this fuckin' minute like!

Tarpey   Watch your tongue over there!

Peter (*doesn't register it*)   Fuckin' human bein's, ain't we? Are and all, Peter. Fuckin' Catholics, so we are.

Tarpey   You, watch your tongue!

Peter   Ay?

Goldfish   Pedro!

Tarpey   And you there beside him! (**Goldfish.**)

Goldfish   . . . *Fuck you!*

Bandleader (*off*)   And the next dance, boys and girls, will be a mixed medley, starting with a quickstep. (*Music, loud.*)

Again, it's difficult to hear what is being said, but we can see it. And see the mêlée starting.

Tarpey *is afraid, but he wants to impress the company and is coming to* **Goldfish**. **Kerrigan** *is intervening, restraining him.* **Goldfish** *is going to* **Tarpey**. **Jimmy** *is intervening, restraining him.* **Peter** *hardly knows what's going on. The jostling and pushing start and* **Louise** *and* **Susanne** *are caught up in it. (As are other people present — if we have them!)*

Tarpey *loses his hat at some point. His image, he feels, is suffering because of this, and he would have it back.*

Christy *will return from his errand to find the scuffle in progress. And* **Bunty** *from his other bar.*

Tarpey   What did you say? (*Coming to* **Goldfish**.)

Goldfish   Fuck You!

Tarpey   What did you say?

Goldfish   *Fuck You!*

Peter   Ay?

Kerrigan   Dick! Dick! Let it pass! Let it pass . . . (*Ad libs, variations.*)

Tarpey   I know who you are!

Peter   Ay?

Jimmy   Ary, Goldfish, let it go and there'll be no more about it! (*Ad libs.*)

Tarpey   I know *him*! (*To* **Kerrigan**.)

Peter   Ay? (*And he will retire to a corner with his bottle in a minute.*)

Kerrigan   Let's go, let's go! Let's leave! . . .

Goldfish   You know me all right! Dick! Dick!

Bunty   What's all this? Goldfish! What's all this, what's going on here? (*Coming in*)

Jimmy   Ary, Goldfish!

Goldfish   Fuck him, man, and all the guards in the town!

Christy *comes in, intervenes, takes charge. He has strength and authority.*

Christy   It's all over! It's all over now! Let out the ladies – Watch the girls! It's all over, Simon – No one here has any problems at all! . . . Has anyone here any problems at all? . . . See! See! (*He finds* **Tarpey**'s *hat and offers it to* **Tarpey**:) It's all over? . . . (**Tarpey** *accepts the hat.*) It's all over. Everyone's going dancing.

Bunty   Finish up now! Glasses! (*Goes out to his other bar.*)

People are preparing to leave. The band across the street is now going into the second leg of the mixed medley, a slow dance.

Tarpey   They go to England and America to hone their criminal skills there.

Christy (*calming* **Goldfish**, *taking him back to his place telling him a funny story.*) Hear the one about the buff-sham swallowed the fly? Well . . .

Kerrigan   Forget the dance, will we go up to the Club?

Bunty (*off*)   Finish up now! Glasses!

Christy (*energy, circling the room, collecting glasses:*)   Whee-hee! Finish up now! Glasses!

Louise   I'm going to the dance. (*For* **Christy**'s *benefit.*)

Christy   Whee-hee! (*Ignoring them.*)

Tarpey (*to* **Susanne**)   A nightcap, Miss de Burca?

Kerrigan   Or two. Susanne, you will.

She will. Though she has been watching **Christy**. *At this stage she would prefer his company.*

People are leaving. **Bunty** *has returned.*

Bunty   Thanks, thanks, thank ye all now, behave yourselves now and enjoy yourselves! Thanks, Inspector!

Tarpey (**Kerrigan** *and* **Susanne** *go out*)   The country would come to a stop if we had those bastards around all the time.

Louise   Goodnight! (**Louise** *leaves.*)

Bunty   Thanks, Louise, goodnight! Here, Christy, a pass to the dance for you: You're a very obliging young fella.

Goldfish   *He* (**Tarpey**) can come in here with his 'hat' and I can't?! (*To* **Bunty**.)

Bunty   (*has the small whiskey ready for him under the counter; gives it to him*). Now. (*And collects the money for it.*) Tell my wife in the box office I said it was all right for you to go in on your own. (*He goes out to his other bar, switching off a light.*)

Goldfish   (*blows a sigh and knocks back his drink*)   See you across in a few minutes.

He adjusts himself, preparatory to leaving; indicates **Peter** *who is in a world of his own in a corner. A small gesture from* **Peter**, *it could be to anyone.*

Goldfish   Don't let's ask for the moon, Pedro, I've had enough. (*He's gone.*)

Christy   Go home, Peter, say hello to the missus.

Peter   (*rises wearily, talking to himself*)   Oh Christ . . . Sweet Christ . . . grant me the grace, to find a small hut, in a lonesome place . . . and make it my abode.

He goes out, staggering against the doorway.

Christy *is getting his jacket from somewhere.* **Susanne** *returns. (She deliberately left something behind, a few minutes ago. She collects it.)*

Susanne   You are joking.

Christy   I'm serious.

Susanne   (*laughs/giggles in a silly, nervous way: she is courting danger?*)   We shall see about that. I am tied up right now with those people out there, otherwise . . . But I could see you tomorrow. Monday.

Christy   Yeh.

Susanne   Evening.

Christy   Yeh.

Susanne   Where?

Christy   I'll call down.

Susanne   Don't call. Let us keep our little tryst a secret.

Kerrigan (*off*)   Susannaaa!

Susanne   Coming! – I've found it! Let us meet in – oh – some romantic private place.

Christy   The wood.

Susanne   Ah, the wood!

Christy   Bend of the river?

Susanne   Right.

Christy   That's on, then.

Susanne   That is on, then.

Christy   Eight o'clock?

Susanne   Five to. (*Leaving:*) Thanks for the drink.

He stands there in the comparative dark for a moment, then he goes out to the dance.

Scene Eight

Tuesday morning, early. **Kerrigan**'*s house.* **Kerrigan**, *standing, looking at a file, from an impressive bundle of files, drinking a morning cup of tea perhaps. Doorbell. He answers it.*

Kerrigan   Oh?! Young Lochinvar has come out of the west! (*He has returned with* **Christy**)   You're up early, could you not sleep?

Christy   Morning.

Kerrigan   What?

Christy *grins/grimaces, foolishly.*

Kerrigan Sit down, can't you see I'm a busy man? What can I do for you?

Christy Don't want to bother, Billy, but!

Christy's *'Morning', above, sounded down. And his grinning and grimacing – his laughing-boy image – aren't functioning that well either. And, unusual for him, his suit is rumpled, he looks dishevelled, like a man who's been up all night. There's something wrong. (There's something gravely wrong.)*

Kerrigan But what? Tuesday, my busiest day! . . . (*Mock casual:*) Enjoyed the dance last Sunday night?

Christy (*foolishly*) Yeh. But last night, I arranged to meet someone. It went badly wrong.

Kerrigan (*begins to groan*) Aw Jesus, not another one of you.

Christy *doesn't understand.*

Kerrigan A favour. A favour, a favour! The town down there – the country – the whole economy is run on favours! And in return you'll give me a goose and a bag of potatoes, will you, for Christmas? What's the problem, what d'you want?

Christy Trouble.

Kerrigan You're in trouble – did you kill someone? – what kind of trouble?

Christy *looks at him, foolishly/eyes dilated/whatever.*

Kerrigan Prick trouble? I knew it. Mrs Burgess, 'Louise'? Doesn't the whole town know it! Devouring married maidens out of season. Do you know that her mother – whatever the extent of that old lady's liberal attitude – isn't a well woman? Haven't you – if her daughter hasn't – any sense of consideration? Or decency or propriety. Why don't the two of you do it in the middle of the Square: that be a good idea? What?

Christy   The charvering stakes has nothing to do with it.

Kerrigan   Oh? 'The charvering stakes', the jiggy-jig stakes. Then what has? Is Michael Burgess going to take a case against you at last?

Christy *shakes his head. But a new thought, a new tack – a way out for him, a solution – has begun to form in his mind.*

Kerrigan   Well, he should. You should be locked up, like what's happening to some of your Paddy-confrères. Do you know that Michael Burgess could have you for assault, enticement, criminal knowledge of his wife? – he could have you on a dozen charges.

Christy *nods.*

Kerrigan   What?

Christy *nods.*

Kerrigan   What?

Christy   Yeh.

Kerrigan   Didn't I warn you about her?

Christy   You were right.

Kerrigan   Oh? Good man!

Christy   A very highly strung neurotic woman, Billy.

Kerrigan   Now! I often wondered what was up with her.

Christy   Well . . . the fact is I decided to pack it in.

Kerrigan   A firm purpose of amendment – Yes?

Christy   She won't agree.

Kerrigan   Irresistible.

Christy   No.

Kerrigan   What? . . . Yes?

Christy *appears to lose the purpose, and calculation, in his 'new tack'. In the following, he becomes confused, goes out of control,* *becomes upset, bewildered and ends in tears.*

Christy   No. I'm tired.

Kerrigan   You're . . . !

Christy   We arranged to meet. 'That's on, then. That is on, then.' Keep it a secret.

Kerrigan   You met. (*Impatient.*)

Christy   To tell her what I was going to do. That I'd come to a decision about it.

Kerrigan   That you were packing it in.

Christy   D'you know what I mean, Billy? That I was serious about it. But that I wanted to be fair. She started to create a scene.

Kerrigan   Hell hath no fury – Splendid!

Christy   No. That she'd stand in my way, she said. Sex, yes, reality, she said, but couldn't – wouldn't – give me a reason why she'd stand in my way – 'No reason!' She became out of control, she became very out of control –

Kerrigan   Christy –

Christy   All over the place – crazy – she started saying terrible things –

Kerrigan   Christy –

Christy   Terrible. Then pulling up her dress – Hand on (*Her crotch.*) – There was no way of dealing with her – Or how to handle it –

Kerrigan   What're we talking about?!

Christy *has become tearful.*

Kerrigan (*to himself*)   Jesus Christ!

Christy (*tearful*)   I'm tired.

Kerrigan (*sighs heavily and gestures at his work. Then:*) And what d'you expect me to do about it?! A thousand and one things to do – Look at all that! (*Work.*) Two court cases in Newcastle later this morning, an auction this afternoon – your 'friends'' place, de Burcas' place – I have to attend that too . . . Christy?!

Christy (*mention of the auction has galvanised him, returned him to his 'new tack'*) Well . . . the fact is, I *have* come to a decision about it.

Kerrigan And *what* can I do about it?

Christy You can. She's been following me around –

Kerrigan Who has?

Christy She drives up and down outside my house –

Kerrigan Who –

Christy All hours! – she *calls* there! – She was there this morning – She said –

Kerrigan Who said, who-are-we-talking about?

Christy . . . Louise. Mrs Burgess. You were right about her. She said she knew I was with another woman last night.

Kerrigan And you were, I suppose. Cursed with an eye for a beautiful woman. Yes, my son, who was she and how many times? Aw, Jesus, Christy, am I a solicitor – State Solicitor, public prosecutor – or a father confessor? Go on.

Christy Now she's threatening –

Kerrigan A bigger scene – Suicide? – Lovely! – Yes?

Christy I told her I was nowhere last night.

Kerrigan Where is that?

Christy Told her I was with no one last night.

Kerrigan Meaning? Is this where I come in? That you were up here with me, painting walls maybe, here, with me?

Christy I told her I was locked up.

Kerrigan   . . . You want me to arrange?

Christy   Well, the fact is, I told her stop watching me, following me, watching the house, that I was with no one. That if she – or anybody else – seen me arrive home six o'clock this morning was because I'd spent the night in the cells, that they'd just released me, that I was locked up. She said prove it then, and she'd step aside. Oh I'll prove it all right I said and she'd step aside all right then because she'd have to, because this was the end of the line. That I'd show her the summons when it was issued to me. (*Shrugs, 'or'.*) Go to the station herself if she liked, look at the records and see my name on them. But that this was it, finito.

Kerrigan   . . . Look at the cut of you. Is that the good suit you had on last week? . . . And you were fighting too the other night, I hear – what's the matter with you?! With your Yankee pal. That Goldfish is an out-and-out troublemaker, a menace. But the guards will deal with him yet. Okay, I'll fix it: I'll have a word with Inspector Tarpey. You were locked up all night last night: drunk and disorderly. (*Sighs.*) I might as well get it over with. I've to drop these down to the station anyway. (*Bundle of files.*) Wait here! Till I come back with your summons. Prick trouble. You're a thundering bollix. (*He leaves.*)

Christy, *alone, a man in a nightmare, but one that he is going to see through to its conclusion.*

Scene Nine

The drawing room half of De Burcas' double room. An occasional table, two chairs, a table lamp.

Mother, **Marie** *and* **Louise** *form an uncomfortable group in the doorway from the hall. They were about to enter but a couple of* **Strangers** *– a man and a woman – are inspecting the room.*

Upstage, the dining room. Blinding sunlight falling on the table – or on one end of it. **Bunty** *is there, arranging things for himself.*

The **Strangers** *have decided to inspect the hall: the de Burcas step aside to let them out the doorway.*

Louise   Oh, excuse me!

Mother   . . . Now we know what it's like. (*She moves towards the dining room but changes her mind: there are other people in there.*)

Marie   Hmm?

Mother   What it's like: not to belong to a place any more.

Marie   Oh I don't know.

Louise   It's still ours!

Mother *to her chair, to consider sitting in it, to decide against it. She flaps her hands. Where to go?*

Marie's *humouring laugh.* **Mother**'s *grin.*

A car arriving outside.

Mother   Is that Susanne? See, Marie. Where is that girl?

Bunty (*comes from the dining room, importantly*)   We'll start now in a minute, ma'am, when Billy Kerrigan arrives.

Marie   He's here.

Bunty *returns to the dining room.*

Mother   I didn't think it'd be like this.

Louise   People traipsing through the house.

Marie   It'll be over in no time. (*To the hall door to meet* **Kerrigan**.) Billy!

Kerrigan (*with his briefcase*)   Marie! Are we all set up? Mrs de Burca!

Bunty (*returning*)   Mr Kerrigan!

Kerrigan   Are we all set up?

Bunty   Not that many of them in there, and some of them are only gawkers.

Kerrigan   Have you set the reserve price?

Bunty (*to* **Mother**)   Two-two-double-o.

Kerrigan   Two thousand two hundred: and you're happy with that?

Mother *nods.*

The **Strangers** *return from the hall and go into the dining room.*

Bunty   Give it another minute.

Louise   The cheek of some people. (*The* **Strangers**.)

Christy *appears in the hall doorway but retreats again when he sees the de Burcas. (They don't see him.)*

Bunty   Ah, it'd be a nice place all right with a bit of work done on it . . . If I can get two of them bidding against each other. Yeh. (*To* **Kerrigan**.) Will we? ('*start*'.)

They are about to go into the dining room.

Mother   But do we have to be here?

Bunty   Aw it'd be better, ma'am. To be near at hand in case a deal comes up or has to be struck. (*And looks at* **Kerrigan** *for support.*)

Kerrigan (*agrees*)   It's usual. (*And goes into the dining room.*)

Bunty   Sit down there for yourself, ma'am, and you can be sure I'm going to do the very best I can for ye. (*He follows* **Kerrigan**.)

Louise   It's like Westland Row Station.

Marie   Perhaps we should have packed our bags?

Mother (*grins; sits*)   Now we know what it's like.

Bunty   All right then, yeh. I'm offering this house for sale, Woodlawn House, private residence on over three acres, and I'll pass ye over now to this gent on my left, 'the man who got there', to give us the 'foresaids and thereuntos.

Kerrigan (*reads from a document*)   I act for the vendor of

this property, Sabina Esther Winifred de Burca who is the
legal Personal Representative of John Louis Ulick de Burca,
deceased [obit. 17/6/1943], and to whom Grant of Probate
of his last Will was granted forth of the Principal Probate
Registry of the High Court on the thirteenth of November
1944.

Mother We're being sentenced.

Marie Mum? . . . Better than a poke in the eye?

Mother We're being sentenced. (*Grins.*)

Marie *grins.* **Louise** *brushes away private tears.*

Kerrigan (*continuous*) The closing date of this sale will be
twenty-one days from the date of purchase. Should the
Purchaser fail to complete the purchase price on that date,
such Purchaser shall bear interest to the date of actual
completion at the rate of eight per centum per annum.

Marie We'll be rich, everybody.

Kerrigan The Particulars and Tenure of the property
are as follows:

Marie Rich.

Kerrigan The property is Woodlawn House in the
townland of Newcastle. It stands on its own grounds
which –

Bunty Where else would it stand? (*Some laughter from the
dining room.*)

Kerrigan It stands on its own grounds which comprise
an area of three acres, one rood and thirty-eight perches
statute measure and is held under two titles as follows:

Mother We're being sent into exile. (*Grins.*)

Marie We'll be rich!

Marie *would shield her mother from what is going on behind them.
She rises / moves in impotent effort. A glance into the dining room as
she does so.*

Mother   I'd no idea it was like this.

Marie (*returning to her place*)   Mum?

Mother *shakes her head; grins.*

Kerrigan (*continuous*)   One. The dwelling house, messuage, hereditaments and premises on one acre, one rood and thirty-eight perches statute measure is held under a Lease for Lives renewable for ever, dated 23/2/1839, subject to covenants on the part of the Lessee and conditions therein contained, at a rent of one peppercorn, if demanded.

Mother   A rent of what?

Marie (*shrugs/grins*)   ... Christy is in there ... I didn't see him arrive, did you?

They didn't.

Kerrigan (*continuous*)   The Lease has not been converted to a Fee Farm Grant pursuant to the provisions of the Renewable Leasehold Conversion Act, 1949, and the Purchaser shall not require the Vendor to effect such conversion.

Bunty   Lookit, one of ye will have the place for ever – That's all. ('*This is a waste of time.*')

Kerrigan   Two. The balance of the lands comprising two acres, known as the 'Wide Ridge', is held in fee simple and is the subject matter of Folio 9927 of the Registry of Freeholders.

Mother *starts to rise through the above and hangs there, half-risen.*

Marie   Mum?

Mother *shakes her head, smiles, sits back in her chair. But she's up again after a moment, to stand, grin:*

Mother   And where is Susanne? Where-is-that-girl? (*Sits again*)

Kerrigan   I will now take any questions which you wish to put to me on the Conditions or on the Title.

Bunty   There ye are now, thereunto, whereas – Any questions?

Mother (*grins*)   This is hell.

Marie   Mum?

Bunty   No questions?

Mother   It's like being sent to hell.

Bunty   I've a question. Where would a man find a peppercorn? (*Some laughter.*)

Kerrigan   Try a peppermill. (*Drily.*)

Bunty   Right then, we'll start . . . Who'll offer me two thousand pounds, two thousand? . . . Two thousand pounds, a modest beginning, who'll start the bidding at two thousand pounds, who'll start me off? . . . For this attractive property . . . Lovely dwelling, standing on its own grounds – (*Which he finds amusing.*) – as our learned friend beside me told us . . . Who'll start me off at nineteen hundred? . . . Eighteen fifty? To start me off . . . Ah, come on, don't be thinking ye're cute! This's a wonderful chance for someone, wonderful property with scenery, a veritable, veritable little Ireland in itself: seventeen hundred and fifty pounds, someone! What an active man with a spade could do to it. Or a tractor'd soon put manners on the two-acre field growing wild up the back there. And a lick of paint to the windows – Seventeen hundred?

Mother *half rises again during the above. She doesn't know what to do with herself.*

Marie   Oh, there are great shenanigans going on in government, in the Dáil.

Mother   Love?

Marie   You didn't read your paper yet today.

Bunty   Who'll start the ball rolling, who wants first blood? Ye're wasting my time and all that lovely sunshine out there . . .

Marie *has risen/moved again, as before.*

Marie   The funniest thing, a big debate about flour.

Mother   Oh?

Marie   Yes!

Mother   For making bread?

Marie   Flour! What a business!

Louise   I heard something about that. What was it again, Marie? (*Encouraging* **Marie**.)

Marie   Well, it seems that the millers were demanding an increase for their flour. This – of-course! – would give the government the problem of allowing the bakers to put up the price of a loaf. But then one clever bod of a politician – a minister – came up with the solution: tell the bakers to take a slice off the loaf of bread.

Mother   Make the loaf smaller?

Marie   Yes! But don't let on to the housewife! . . . I dare not think how it's all going to end.

Bunty (*continuous*)   If you're not in you can't win – seventeen hundred pounds . . . Ladies and gentlemen, it's twenty-nine minutes past two o'clock, ye heard the et ceteras and so forths and everything is clean – start me off, start me off – Start! – At seventeen hundred pounds – and this place is going to be somebody's for ever and ever and ever, yeh amen, for eternity. That's what them big words meant.

Mother *rises.*

Marie   Mum?

Mother   I'll go to my room, Marie.

Marie   Yes.

Mother   Don't you have power-of-attorney over everything, and if anything comes up –

Marie 'A deal' –

Mother 'A deal', can't you 'deal' with it? (*Both of them grinning, going off.*) And she (**Susanne**) was out 'til all hours on Sunday night.

Louise She was up in the Club.

Mother Wherever she's got herself to last night.

Marie I'll be back in a minute.

*She follows **Mother** out of the room.*

Bunty Well, I don't know what this shy company is thinking, but take a care ye don't let yere shyness and cleverality get the better of ye now and miss yere chance, because I have my instructions and I'll withdraw the sale entirely. So, do I have an *opening* bid? No offers? No takers? . . . Does no one want it? Before I withdraw it . . . And that'll be all right too: because I'll find a stranger for it, a foreigner. Or a Dublin man. And see how fast they'll jump at it. (*He looks at **Kerrigan**. **Kerrigan** shrugs.*) That's it, then: I'm withdrawing the –

Christy *interrupts. A clown: a laugh in his voice:*

Christy Excuse me!

Bunty Who's that? I can't see you with the sun.

Christy Simon!

Bunty Christy?

Christy That's me!

Bunty Did you want something?

Christy Can I ask a question of you?

Bunty What? – are you making a bid? We're holding an auction here, not a-a-a –

Christy Isn't there a reserve price on it?

Bunty What?

Christy   What's the reserve price exactly?

Bunty (*dismisses the question and* **Christy**)   No one wants it then? All right, I now withdraw the –

Christy   Two thousand four hundred!

Bunty   Two?

Christy   Two thousand four hundred!

Bunty   Two?

Christy   Two thousand four hundred!

Bunty   Two thousand four hundred pounds?

Christy   Two – two thousand four hundred pounds – Are you deaf, Sim-on? That's what I said! Anybody else? (*He's inviting others to bid higher.*)

Bunty   Excuse me! –

Christy   Anybody else?!

Bunty   Excuse me – Christy! – excuse me there! Are you making a bid?

Christy   Are you stupid or what?! I just did! I just made a bid! Sim-on!

Bunty   It's a serious business making –

Christy   Oh the money will be there! Don't fret your head about that! Sim-on! Two thousand four hundred is maybe my first bid! – Anybody else here? You ask them. I thought you were meant to be running this shebang.

Bunty   I'm offered two thousand four hundred pounds for Woodlawn. Is there any advance on that? . . . As the reserve price has been met, and if there's no advance on it? . . . Going once, twice . . . sold to – Sold.

Louise *leaves to bring the news to* **Mother** *and* **Marie**.

We see **Christy** *sign a document for* **Bunty** *on the dining-room table.*

The **Strangers**, *from the top of the scene, reappear and leave.*

Bunty, *with the document that* **Christy** *signed,* **Christy** *and* **Kerrigan** *come to the drawing room.*

Bunty   We'll get Mrs de Burca's signature on this now.

Christy   Mrs de Burca? Well, I've signed it. I mean, I'm not needed now, am I? Know what I mean? So I'll be off. I'd arranged, actually – Yeh know! (*He's gone – as if to keep an appointment.*)

Bunty (*bemused*)   This's one for the book!

Kerrigan *is puzzled too, but he's smiling, smirking.*

Bunty   Where would he get money like that?

Kerrigan   Where did you get yours?

Marie *is coming in.*

Bunty   Now: did I do well for ye?!

Marie   Has he gone?

Kerrigan   You can sign that, Marie.

Marie (*signs the document*)   I was afraid some Tom, Dick or Harry would buy it.

Scene Ten

Bunty's. *Evening – Night. A sing-song. A celebration – Revelry.* **Christy** *is a hero and he's behaving like one. He is drunk, calling the tune, abandoned. He wants to become drunker. (But he has street sense too, cunning. And there are extremes of mood swings.) Other emigrants are present. As are* **Goldfish** *and* **Peter**, *whose arm is in a sling.* **Bunty**. *And* **Kerrigan**, *who does not integrate with anyone.*

A ragged, laughing chorus of voices before and as the lights come up, singing: 'A-round the corner – Oo-oo!/Beneath the berry tree/A-round the footpath, behind the bush/Looking for Henry Lee.'

Christy   Martin! ('*Sing*'.)

Goldfish   'Tonight all the folks'll cut the corn –'

All   'Cut the corn!'

Goldfish   'Tonight I'll be glad that I was born –'

Christy   Same again in that, Simon! (*He has drained his glass.*) –

Goldfish   'For my Henry Lee I'll see/He'll come cuttin' corn with me/And we'll meet neath the bitter berry tree.'

Christy   A-round the corner! (*A shout.*)

All   Oo-oo! 'Beneath the berry tree/A-round the footpath, behind the bush/Lookin' for Henry Lee!'

Applause, together with:

Peter   A-round the corner, Khrisht!

Bunty   (*drink to* **Christy**)   Some man, some man!

Peter   Fair ol' dos, Khrisht, all right like!

Christy   Do a round! For the house, Simon!

Bunty   D'yeh hear that, Mr Kerrigan?

Christy   Gentle when stroked, fierce when provoked!

Goldfish   Hee-haw!

Peter   Gentle when stroked, Khrisht!

Bunty   Same again over there, is it, Mr Kerrigan?

Kerrigan *shakes his head.*

Bunty   Why wouldn't yeh? The squire is treating us again!

Christy   And have one yourself, Simon!

Bunty   Jesus Christ, England is a great country for some –

Christy   Another song! Someone! –

Bunty   And me now, I slaved for seven years abroad in

Dagenham and I end up back here a bigger slave – a waitress – serving drink for the new gentry! (*Laughter – everything is a laugh.*)

Christy (*singing*)   'I think that I shall never see/A poem lovely as a tree/A tree that looks at God all day/And lifts her leafy arms to pray –'

Jimmy *has come in, excited, in his boiler suit.*

Jimmy   Where is he?

Christy   Jim-ee! 'A tree that may in summer wear/A nest of robins in her hair!'

Jimmy   Put it there, Christy – How can you buy Killarney! I only just heard it!

Christy   And a pint for Jimmy!

Jimmy   But I always knew it!

Christy   Or a short, Jimmy?

Jimmy   Pint, Christy, thanks – Pint, Simon! No better man, one of our own sure!

Bunty   Some men, some men!

Peter   Heigh-up, Jimmy mate!

Jimmy   Heigh-up, Peter! I hear y'have it in for the buff-shams' bicycles, Goldfish?

Goldfish   Frankenstein strikes back! (*Whips out a paper, a summons to appear in court*)   Says I'm to appear afore the magistrate come Toosday, twenty-eight [28th] for a-rustlin' short-horn Raleighs.

Peter   I've one too like! (*Produces his summons.*)

Goldfish   Yo's t'appear afore Judge Roy Bean as well?

Peter   John P. Hogan's window. Staggerin' home like, and I went like this like, and fell through the . . .

Jimmy   Yeh hoor yeh, Peter!

Christy   I love the smell of broken glass! (*Producing his summons.*) Me too, last night.

Peter   Last night, ay?

Goldfish   What they get you on?

Christy   Tell you again – 'A-round the corner?!'

Others   'Oo-oo'!

Bunty   Squire! (*Calling* **Christy** *to hand the drinks round.*)

Christy (*collecting drinks; calls*)   Peter, yourself, a song! Have another, Billy!

Kerrigan *shakes his head.* (*There's something bugging him, not making sense.*)

Peter (*singing*)   'A mother's love's a blessing/No matter where you roam' –

Bunty   Jesus Christ, another comeallyeh! –

Peter   'Keep her while she's living/You'll miss her when she's gone' –

Christy   Your pint is on the way, Jimmy! –

Jimmy   No better man, Christy! –

Peter   'Love her as in childhood/Though feeble, old and grey' –

Bunty   Someone else! –

All   'For you'll never miss a mother's love/Till she's buried beneath the clay.'

Applause, together with:

Bunty   Someone else! –

Christy (*pint to* **Jimmy**)   Jimmy!

Jimmy   May the hand never falter! Give us one yourself, Christy – I think that I shall never see!

Christy   Nah.

Bunty   Someone else quick, or he'll only start up again! –

Peter   Or yourself, Bunty! –

Goldfish   'Wanting you, every night I am wanting you' – Chris! –

Peter   Or Mr Kerrigan?!

Jimmy   Here in my heart, Christy!

Peter   Mr Kerrigan, poetry like!

Christy   Billy!

Peter   Mr Kerrigan!

Bunty   Sure people without any education at all can quote poetry without making a boast of it! (*He winks behind* **Kerrigan**'s *back.*)

Christy (*taking a drink to* **Kerrigan**)   Here, Billy, go on, have another!

Kerrigan (*'no'*)   I'm late as it is. See yeh.

Christy   When do I sign the deeds?

Kerrigan   Must wait due process, Christopher: you heard me yourself. (*Leaving; turns back.*) Where'd you get the money?

Christy, *as in Scene Three, a 'fiddling clown'. And a laugh from others.*

Kerrigan   But there's *something* not making sense.

Bunty   No poetry, then, for us tonight?

Christy   Thanks, Billy! (**Kerrigan** *is leaving.*)

Bunty   Goodnight to yeh now, Mr Kerrigan!

Kerrigan   What? (*To* **Bunty***:*) At very best, you're an ignorant little man. (*He's gone.*)

Bunty *laughs after him. Others are laughing drunkenly. And*

Christy, *throwing money to* **Bunty**, *breaks into sudden abandoned song.*

Christy 'Here in my heart I'm so lone and oh so lonely,/Here in my heart I just long for you only,/Here in my heart . . .'

Marie *has come in. (Gone unnoticed for a moment or two.) He sees* **Marie** *and stops his song. A vague smile — some kind of melancholy, is it, or remorse? And is there some strange connection between him and this woman? She comes to him.*

Marie My mother was keen that I should see you. We heard you had to dash. She asked me to tell you that she's delighted, and to wish you luck. (*He nods, soberly. Then he bows to her.*) And so am I, very pleased. (*She offers her hand.*)

Christy (*takes it. Then kisses it*) Will you have a drink with me, Marie?

Marie Yes, please.

Christy A drink for Miss de Burca, Simon. Whatever she wants.

Bunty What would you like, Marie? (*He tends her.*)

Goldfish Here in my heart, Chris!

Jimmy I'm so lone and so lonely, Christy!

Christy (*takes* **Marie**'s *hand? Sings*) 'When the scented night of summer covers/Field and city with her veil of blue/All the lanes are filled with straying lovers/Murmuring the words I say to you:/Just a little love, a little kiss/Just an hour that holds a world of bliss/Eyes that tremble like the stars above me/And the little words that say':

Goldfish/Christy 'You love me.'

Bunty (*going off*) You love me, yeh.

Peter Night will pass. (*Gently.*)

Christy 'Night will pass and day will follow after/Other griefs and joys will come with day/Yet through all the

weeping and the laughter/You will ever hear the words I
say:/Just a little love, a little kiss/I would
give you all my life for this/As I hold you fast and bend
above you/And I hear you whispering, I love you.'

Applause. Out of which a cacophony develops. As it does, **Tarpey**
comes in, in civvies. He calls/beckons **Marie** *to him and talks
quietly to her. It is clear that he is imparting bad news. And they
leave together.*

*The cacophony grows through the above: from applause to calls for
more, to a* **Christy** *shout 'A-round the corner!' to 'Oo-oos!' of
replies and laughter, to four singers coming in on top of each other,
progressively, with four different songs: Until, eventually, and to the
end of the scene, four different songs are being sung simultaneously.*

Peter 'Oh father dear, I oft-times hear you speak of
Erin's Isle . . .' (*Etc.*)

Jimmy (*comes in with his song*) 'While the mission bells
were ringing, calling for thee evening prayer . . .' (*Etc.*)

Goldfish (*coming in now with his*) 'Carolina, gave me Dinah
. . . Dinah, is there anyone finah/In the State of Carolina
. . .' (*Etc. – Eddie Cantor style – vibrant.*)

And **Christy,** *who has observed – soberly –* **Marie** *leave with*
Tarpey *– now punches the air defiantly, stomps the floor and joins
the cacophony with a fourth song:*

Christy 'Here in my heart I'm alone and so lonely/Here
in . . .' (*Etc.*)

Scene Eleven

It's a few days later. Night. De Burcas'.

*In the drawing room, one lamp, the table lamp, is lit on the
occasional table. (The vacuum of the dining room is upstage.)*
Mother *in mourning clothes is seated in one chair and* **1st
Woman** *is in the other. With them, standing, is* **1st Man**.
Louise *comes from the dining room with a tray to offer small
glasses of drink.*

Susanne *has been buried today and sympathisers still call to pay their respects, stay for a little, drink the ritual drink and leave again. (Movement is silent, conversation hushed, sibilant: something almost dreamlike.)*

Marie *receives visitors at the door. The occupants of a car are arriving:*

2nd Woman   Marie, dear, so sorry, so sorry.

Marie   Mrs Hession.

2nd Man   Sorry for your trouble.

Marie   Mr Hession. (*She ushers them to* **Mother**.) Mum? Mrs Hession. Mr Hession.

2nd Woman   Sabina, Sabina, so sorry, so sorry.

Mother   Thank you, thank you.

2nd Woman   Louise, Louise, so sorry, so sorry.

Louise *is inclined to be tearful, nods her thanks and goes off with her tray.* **1st Man** *and* **1st Woman** *vacate their places in favour of* **2nd Man** *and* **2nd Woman**.

2nd Man   Sorry for your trouble.

Mother   Thank you, thank you.

2nd Woman   When did it happen?

Mother   Last Monday night.

2nd Woman   And she was buried today.

Mother   There had to be a post-mortem. You know. So she wasn't buried until today.

2nd Woman   So young.

Mother   Yes.

*The lights of a second car (**Bunty**'s) washing the place. (A third car will arrive shortly.)*

2nd Woman   We never know the time or the place. But she's in heaven now. (*And indistinguishable whispers of the kind: 'And did you hear about the fall Molly Larkin had? She was coming down the stairs . . .'*)

Louise (*returning with a drink for them*)   Mr Hession. Mrs Hession.

2nd Woman   Thank you. (*A whisper.*)

2nd Man   Thank you. (*A whisper.*)

Marie *is receiving* **Bunty** *and ushering him to her mother.*

Bunty   Sorry again for your trouble, Marie.

Marie   Thank you. Mr Tierney, Mum.

Bunty   Sorry for your trouble, ma'am.

Mother   Thank you, thank you.

Bunty   Sorry for your trouble, Louise.

Louise   Thank you. (*And goes off again to dining room.*)

Marie   Mum? (*She has fetched a footstool which she would like*
Mother   *to use.*)

Mother *smiles her thanks but declines it.* **1st Man** *and* **1st Woman** *are leaving. More handshakes.*

1st Woman   So sorry again.

Mother   Thank you, thank you.

1st Man   So sorry.

Mother   Thank you, thank you.

Marie (*ushers them out*)   Thank you for calling.

1st Woman   So sorry.

Marie (*handshakes*)   Thank you. Thank you.

They leave. As they do so, a muted 'Goodnight' to **Kerrigan** *and* **Tarpey** *who are coming in to join* **Marie**. **Tarpey** *is in uniform.*

Kerrigan Marie. (*Simply a nod.*)

Tarpey Miss de Burca. We got the final reports and everything is consistent with its being an accident. We thought you should know. It's been gone into and there's no other explanation.

Marie She slipped.

Tarpey Yes. Or tripped, falling into the shallows. And the rocks there. (*Meaning that her head hit the rocks.*) The path is uneven at that spot and close to the bank, and there are overground roots there. We thought you should know. It stops the imagination.

Marie Oh dear, I don't understand it. (*She frowns. The explanation doesn't make sense to her. She smiles:*) But I know that this is – Beyond your call of duty? And we appreciate it. (*Handshake:*) You're very kind. (*Handshake:*) Billy.

Tarpey If there's anything further, Miss de Burca, that we can do.

Marie Thank you.

Tarpey But you have plenty of friends.

Marie Not that many.

'Not that many': she is smiling bravely but she nearly cracks on the line. She ushers them to **Mother**.

Mum? (*And she retires to the dining room to deal with her emotion there.*)

Tarpey Mrs de Burca. (*Handshake.*)

Mother Thank you, thank you.

Kerrigan Mrs de Burca.

Mother Thank you, thank you.

Tarpey We got the final reports and everything is consistent with it being an accident. (*He sits beside her.*) We thought you should know.

Mother Thank you, thank you.

2nd Man and **2nd Woman** *have vacated their places –*
marginally – in favour of **Tarpey** *and* **Kerrigan**. *All, including*
Bunty, *form a circle around* **Mother**. *And* **Louise** *is arriving*
with her tray of drinks. (As appropriate, they sympathise with
Louise.)

And **Christy** *arrives in the doorway, is rooted there, mouth open at*
the hushed party, unnoticed as yet. (He has been lurking outside in the
grounds for some time, wondering if he dares face mother.) In a
moment, when he will speak the formulaic words – 'I'm sorry for
your trouble, Marie' – his voice comes out too loud, thus causing
heads of other visitors to turn momentarily in his direction.

Marie *sees him, hurries to him eagerly, emotionally.*

Marie Christy!

Christy I'm sorry for your trouble, Marie! (*Offering a*
handshake.)

But her arms are around him, indeed, she clings to him like a woman
seeking and finding shelter in a brother – or a husband.

Marie Oh Christy! Oh Christy! I thought you weren't
going to call.

Christy . . . Marie? (*He's confused at this woman whom he*
considered to be aloof and disapproving.)

Marie I've been waiting. I've been wondering where you
were. (*Releases him.*) I thought you weren't going to call.

Christy No.

Marie (*tears of gratitude; love. She smiles*) Thank you. Come
in, come in!

She is ushering him to **Mother**.

As she does so, **Kerrigan** *removes himself from* **Mother**'*s group,*
moves aside quietly. He would avoid **Christy**. *(He's a worried*
man, worried for his own survival. His misgivings about the course of
events that have happened are great.)

Marie Mum? (*Presenting him.*) Christy. (*And she retires.*)

Mother *smiles, holds out her hands to him.*

Christy Mrs de Burca. (*A tentative bow.*)

And he steps back out of the circle to remove himself from them. He finds himself beside **Kerrigan**.

Christy Billy. (*He doesn't know where to move.*)

Louise *comes to them with her tray.*

Louise Billy? ('*A drink.*')

Kerrigan No thank you.

Louise Christy?

Christy Actually, in a bit of bother myself, Louise: I'm up in court next week. Yeh know?

Louise I'm sorry for your trouble. (*Coldly. And she leaves them.*)

Christy (*grins foolishly. Then:*) Yeh going for a drink or anything on the way home?

Kerrigan It was her you were with last Monday night?

Christy . . . Yeh?

Kerrigan Louise. I don't care where you got the money to buy the house, but doubts are springing something terrible about this other matter. It was her, Louise, Mrs Burgess, that you were with. Wasn't it?

Christy *gestures/shrugs, and nods ambivalently. Wary.*

Kerrigan No games – I'm the bright lad in this town. It took me some doing to get where I am: I had to play some games with them to get out of Barrack Street. And I'm not going back there. Or to any place worse. I belong here now. I asked you a question.

Christy Your conscience, Bil-ly! D'yeh know what I mean? I'm sorry that you're up there, so high.

Kerrigan   I asked you a question.

Christy   Why don't you ask *her*?

Kerrigan   I've hung myself out to dry for you, fixing you up with that bogus charge for last Monday night. That bogus charge is in the records now, written down, countersigned, sent out to the district court. It was Louise you were with, not somebody else – that's all I'm asking?

Christy (*shrugs/gestures that 'he's sorry but what can he do', and*)   Was locked up all night last Monday night, Billy.

All the visitors are preparing to leave. **Tarpey** *is shaking hands with* **Mother**. **Louise** *(who has been out of the room, briefly) is putting on her coat.* **2nd Woman** *comes to* **Kerrigan** *and* **Christy** *to shake hands with them, briefly.*

2nd Woman   Sad occasion. Sad occasion.

Kerrigan *returns to* **Mother**'*s group, to bow:*

Kerrigan   Mrs de Burca.

Mother   Thank you, thank you.

Tarpey   Miss de Burca. (*Shakes hands with* **Marie**.)

Marie   Thank you. (*She sees* **Tarpey** *and* **Kerrigan** *to the door.*)

Louise   I'm going home for a while, Mum.

Mother   Do, love, do. Go to bed, have a rest.

Louise *kisses* **Mother** *and joins* **Marie** *at the door for a whisper before leaving.*

Mother *sees* **Christy** *across from her, his unease, her hand out in invitation.*

Mother   Christy. (*He comes to her.*)

2nd Woman   So sorry again, Sabina, I'm so sorry.

Mother   Thank you, thank you. Sit beside me, Christy.

He sits. (Perhaps he chooses the footstool rather than the second chair.)

2nd Woman   But she's at peace now.

Mother   Thank you, thank you.

2nd Man   So sorry.

Mother   Thank you, thank you.

2nd Woman (*and* **2nd Man**, *being shown out by* **Marie**)   She's with God now, where we'll all be one day after all our wanderings and searchings . . .

Marie *goes off with them.*

Bunty   What can we say, ma'am?

Mother   Thank you, thank you.

Bunty   What can we say, yeh. (*A nod:*) Christy. (*And he leaves.*)

Mother (*smiles, contains a sigh*)   Give me a cigarette, Christy.

Marie (*off*)   Thank you again.

Bunty (*off*)   Goodnight, Marie.

Marie (*off*)   Goodnight.

The final two cars driving away.

During the above, **Christy** *has given* **Mother** *a cigarette. (He is in the other chair now.) She is exhausted but she sees that he is troubled and she's caring of him. He sees her as a woman of great strength and understanding. He has something to confess.*

Christy   Mrs de Burca, I've something to tell you.

Mother   Christy? . . . And of course there are things we have to talk about. Things that should have been but weren't mentioned at the auction. (*A puff of the cigarette.*) The gravity-fed water supply to the house gives trouble. D'you know? The second filter on the line gets blocked with leaves and things. But another day's work for us. (*Another puff.*) The lead in the valleys of the roof, I believe, is porous. We'll list those things and come to some arrangement with you about them. (*Another puff of the cigarette and she gives it to him to extinguish it for her, smiling.*) Thank you. And we'll start getting our things together, packing. And have the place nice for you. (*And she sighs the sigh she has been containing.*) Yes, she's at home now, she's at peace, it's over.

Christy (*'No': he shakes his head to himself.*) I've something to tell you. I'm sorry, I'm so sorry, I'm sorry.

Mother Christy?

Christy Always admired this family, but I'm afraid I let you down. And I'd give anything to put it right with you. And I wish now I'd come and talked to you direct. Told you, since you were bent on selling, hook or crook, I was going to buy it. I'd have the money. That it couldn't be the thing at all to let some Tom, Dick or Harry in: they don't *know*. They'd spoil it in a month. That I wanted it: I don't know why that should be, but I'm surer of it now than ever. No matter what happens. But if I'd came and talked to you direct, it might've looked like I was trying to get round you. Everyone is trying to pull a fast one these days. And at the same time I'm doing the wall, jobs about the place, you thanking me and I've started standing there, looking at you dumb. And at the same time I didn't want, when I bought it, it to come as a shock. And that was my mistake. Susanne. I talked to her ... And they're on to it I was with her in the wood: [I'm] nearly sure of it. But they don't know how to jump or can't. (*He brushes away, dismisses all authority.*) In any case, they don't matter, they don't care. Least, I don't think they do ... So we arranged to meet in the wood. Susanne. Told her my plan, so that when the time came she'd explain to you that she knew it in advance. Told her my plan, that I was going to buy it, that that way it'd always be here, for her, for you, for everyone, that otherwise a great mistake was being made. She said she knew things about me, how I made a living, things I was up to over there. (*London.*) Maybe she did know. How therefore could I even dream of here. She said ... Yes, maybe I've been up to things, the other side, things I wouldn't care to mention, not to you, Mrs de Burca: But strange as it may seem, that's all the more reason why a person does: Dream. It's no more strange than a child without a tosser in his pocket wanting to possess the setting sun going down out there ... I said it's up for sale. She said my mother scrubbing your floors. I said did she want it? (*Shakes his head: she didn't.*) But I'd be the last one to have it, face reality. She ... (*Offered him sex but he cannot tell this to* **Mother**.) Reality? ... She became very out of hand in every way. She said choice things. There was nothing I could do. She kept on, and I don't think there was anything I could do, and that's on my solemn and dying oath. And – (*His fist: how he hit her.*) And she ... (*Fell backwards and fell into the river.*) I hit her, Mrs de Burca ... Mrs de Burca. Don't tell.

Mother   ... I won't tell. I won't tell anyone.

His whispered confidence/confession alarmed her at the start. Now she's shattered, finished.

He leaves. (He may be tired/whatever, but he isn't finished.)

She emits a single moan. Her heart is broken.

The lights fading. **Marie** *comes in to look out the window.*

Mother   I'd like to go to bed now.

Scene Twelve

Bunty's. *Afternoon. A few days later.* **Peter** *is drinking a glass of ale, in silence. His suitcase is somewhere nearby.* **Christy** *is sitting over a half-drunk pint of Guinness. (Just sitting over it.)*

Peter   ... Ever work with the diddicoys over there, Khrisht? ... English tinkers like ... They drink tea and all ... (*He's sensitive – to his capacity – to* **Christy**'s *mood.*)

Goldfish *comes in with his suitcase. He has dropped the American vocabulary.*

Peter   Ay? (*Referring to the suitcase.*)

Goldfish   This fucking place is getting on my nerves.

Peter   I thought you had another week?

Goldfish (*calls*)   Bottle of Time there! I'll go back like everyone else today, at least as far as Dublin, see if I can do something about the date on my ticket. Get back to the U.S. of A.

Peter   Ay like?

Goldfish   Don't know where I am in this town.

Peter   How much the judge get you for?

Goldfish   Aw fuck it.

Peter   He fine you a pound, Khrisht?

Christy   Yeh.

Goldfish   When – where! – did this drunk and disorderly caper of yours happen?

Christy   Ah yeh.

Peter   He got me for two quid, the fine like. It would've been more but I told him –

Goldfish   I don't know who I am.

Peter   And nine for John P. Hogan's window. But that was only fair.

The rolls of money are no longer in evidence. **Goldfish** *is counting coins to pay for his drink.* **Bunty** *is coming in, pouring the bottle of Time.*

Goldfish   'People from this town are decent respectable hard-working people', Simon?

Peter   Ay?

Goldfish   That's what he said to me, the judge. 'I don't know where you come from but in this town we respect private property.'

Bunty   They do in their arses.

Goldfish   'And it's my business to see that the likes of you and your kind back from England respects it too.'

Bunty   And the law and the guards are no good, they only catch what suits them. (*Takes* **Goldfish**'*s coins and goes off.*) Where's all yer big rolls of money now, where have ye them hid?

Goldfish *sighs over the judge, and drinks.*

Peter (*sympathetically*)   How much he get you for?

Goldfish (*to himself*)   Fucking cat. 'Hold your horses there, your honour, two points of fact. One: I'm not come from England, I come all the way back from the United States of America. Two –' 'Take your hands out of your pockets!' 'Two: I'm *from* this town –'

Peter   But you should've –

Goldfish   'You, Your Honour, sir, from my knowledge, is the one that's not.' (*He's*) Another buff-sham from down there Tipperary ways. Twelve pounds fine, forty – forty! – for contempt of court, or two weeks in Limerick. Tarpey – oh you can be sure – *Dick*, had a hand in it all. And thirty-six pounds ten and six for committing grievious bodily harm to four of the buff-shams' bicycles and getting the shit bet (*beaten*) out of me. And kicked to death only for him. (**Christy**.)

Peter   But you should've said you was off today. That's the best one. That's what I told him. When they do hear you're leaving they do even sometimes dismiss the case altogether. Providing you're leaving like.

Bunty (*returning with change, for* **Goldfish** *– a coin*)   And if you voice an honest word of suspicion about anything they don't want to hear, they're fast enough to ask you if you want a slap in the face of a libel suit. Or maybe accuse you of treason. (*He's gone again.*) Yeh.

Christy'*s shoulders are shaking. Perhaps he found the last funny.*

Peter   No but, the missus is gone down there now ahead

of me, to the station like, with the other cases and the
kiddies: I can tell you she had a jolly nice time, mate.

Goldfish   Cat, mouse, pus, corruption. (*He.*) Doesn't know
where I come from. (*He flicks/pitches his coin change into a
corner of the floor.*)

Peter   Well, I had three hundred and ninety pounds,
saved up like for coming home, and if I've a penny of it
left in my pocket when we hit Brum, Snowhill Station, six
o'clock tomorrow morning, I'll be a disappointed man.

Jimmy *comes in in his boiler suit.*

Jimmy   Men!

Peter   Heigh-up, Jimmy!

Jimmy   All roads out there leading to the train. I'm on
the dinner break but I couldn't let ye go without saying
goodbye.

Peter   We have another few minutes. (*Looking at his watch.*)

Jimmy   Ye have a nice day for it anyway. I heard the
judge cut the two legs from under you in the courthouse,
Goldfish?

Goldfish   How would you like to hop around the floor
on your balls? (*No challenge in it.*)

Bunty (*returning*)   Did you want something, Jimmy?

Jimmy   No, I'm grand, I'm fine.

Peter   Aw give the man a drink. Can't you see he has
the lip on him. (*He produces his money: say two pounds, two
notes.*) Khrisht, Goldfish?

They decline.

Jimmy   Small one, Simon. Thanks, Peter.

Bunty *goes off with one of* **Peter**'s *pounds.*

Peter   All the same, I'm looking forward to it, going back
and all, and see how Davy got on, me mate like. But the

one and only thing bothers me: he's always telling jokes
and cracking smart ones, Davy, and I don't get them – Ay?
But strange like, it's quare: I don't think Davy understands
them either.

Bunty *returns with a whiskey for* **Jimmy** *and brandies for* **Peter**
and **Goldfish**.

Bunty   Jimmy. (*Change to* **Peter**.) Now, Peter: I only took
for Jimmy's small one out of that. This one's on the house:
first and last drink of the season.

Peter   Bunty, you're a decent man.

Bunty   Here, Goldfish, don't let it choke yeh.

Goldfish   I don't want your drink.

Bunty   Oh? (*Leaves the drink, moves off again.*) Drink up now
or ye'll miss the train.

Jimmy   Ah drink it up.

Goldfish   Did *I* order that?

Jimmy   Well, luck men whatever! God bless, safe journey!

Peter   Jimmy, mate!

Goldfish (*to* **Christy**)   Hah? What's up?

Christy *gestures 'nothing'.*

Goldfish   Your pretty brown eyes is telling me lies –
What's up? Some young one you've up the pole? I'll stay –
I will – for a day or two if you want, (*and*) say I done her
too.

Christy *shakes his head.*

Jimmy   Oh, did you hear, Christy, Mrs de Burca was
taken to hospital?

Goldfish   What's up?

Christy's *shoulders are shaking again. Perhaps he finds*
Goldfish's *earnestness amusing? (He doesn't. He has heard*
Jimmy's *news about Mrs de Burca; he has heard more than that.)*

Peter (*drink finished, it's time to go*) Well, comrades? You wont come down to the station with us, Khrisht?

Christy Nah.

Peter Bunty, we're off!

Jimmy I'll throw your case on the carrier of my bike out there, Peter, and wheel it down for you.

Peter Sound as a bell, Jimmy.

Goldfish (*to* **Peter**) I'll see you down there. ('*He'll follow.*')

Peter *shakes hands with* **Bunty**, *who has returned, and with* **Christy**.

Peter Finest little fuckin' town in the world this – God bless. (*A handshake. And another.*) God bless. I wouldn't choose a king's ransom. Thanks for everything, fair fuckin' dos, I'd a smashin' fuckin' time and I'll see ye all again next year please God.

He leaves, following **Jimmy** *and his suitcase.*

Bunty Are you drinking this, Goldfish?

Goldfish I'm not, Bunty.

Bunty That's all right then too. (*Goes off, taking the brandy with him.*)

Goldfish The sweet nature of that man.

Christy I sign the deeds of that place couple weeks' time.

Goldfish What?

Christy Mrs de Burca's place. That place I bought off Mrs de Burca.

Goldfish . . . Fuck that place.

Christy Nah, heaven on earth, Mrs de Burca's place.

Goldfish There's something up with you. Fuck that aul fuckin' house, fuck here! We're bigger than here, we're – the energy! They're all old – even the young ones! Fuckin'

place is dyin' – Dead! Junior fuckin' footballers – Fuck
them and their prayers for emigrants. Hop on a train with
me, *now*, take ourselves away out of here, we'll spend a few
days round Dublin, work out a plan for the two of us –
Yeh! – something really interesting! Yeh? Yeh, Chris, yeh!
. . . I'd die for yeh!

Christy (*'nah'*)   Mrs de Burca's place, I bought it off Mrs
de Burca. I have to sign them deeds, finalise the matter.

Goldfish (*shrugs*)   Well. (*Reverts to his American accent:*) I gotta
go, man. Build up these goddamn muscles. Got me a date
with Jersey Joe, Madison Square Gardens, coupla weeks
from now.

Christy (*silently*)   Oh! (*Slips some money to* **Goldfish**.)

Goldfish   . . . Y'all right, sham? I'm askin' yeh!

Christy (*feints – mock pugilistics – throws a few punches.
And:*)   See yeh.

Goldfish (*leaves with his suitcase. Off*)   Move 'em out, hee-
haw!

Bunty (*returning, sipping the brandy*)   . . . You miss them all
the same . . . Don't yeh? . . . But we won't see Goldfish
again. Yeh, I've seen it before. (*He's about to go off again.
Then:*) Did I hear Jimmy Toibin say Mrs de Burca was
taken to hospital? It's worse than that. She's gone, the
creature.

He goes out.

Christy, *alone, his back to us, head bowed, his shoulders shaking.*
(*He's crying.*)

Scene Thirteen

*A few weeks later. Late afternoon. Garden furniture (as in Scene
One). A bag or small suitcase on one of the garden chairs
(**Christy**'s). 'Trees' from the house sung by Arthur Tracy. Some
smoke from a fire off. There are cardboard boxes stacked somewhere*

(and maybe a piece of furniture): **Louise***'s things. And a suitcase* **(Marie***'s).*

Louise *comes in, as from her car, for another box.*

Christy *(calls)*   Are you sure I can't give you a hand?

Louise   You're grand! *(Going out with a box.)*

Christy *is about the place; restless. Eager and apprehensive.*
Marie *from the house, hauling a sack (for the fire), taking the opposite direction to* **Louise**.

Marie   *More* stuff for burning!

Christy   Hah! . . . Are you sure I can't give you –

Marie   'You're grand!' *(She's returning, having slung the bag off.)*

Christy   Arthur Tracy!

Marie   Hm? *(She stops.)*

Christy   I used to think that was your father singing.

Marie   Oh! *(And laughs.)* I thought we'd have some music while we're waiting. Why not! *(Then, the afternoon:)* Glorious! Isn't it? *(And, en route to the house, to* **Louise***, who has returned:)* How are you managing?

Louise *whistles – mock gaiety and a mock stagger – going out again with another load.*

Marie *from the house with another sack:*

Marie   Heigh-ho! *(She slings it off.)* We're nearly there. *(She stops.)* You're staying here tonight, aren't you – Is that all you brought with you? *(The bag. She laughs.)* You haven't changed your mind, have you?

Christy   No.

Marie *(moving again)*   He'll be here in a minute. *(And meets* **Louise***.)*

Louise *(returning)*   My car is full to the gills, so it won't take much more. That was a clever thing to say. This rubbish of mine. Was there ever such – stuff! I'd forgotten about most of it. How it accumulates!

Marie   And Mum's papers, and clothes. Oh dear. (*And she becomes tearful.*)

Christy *watching them, remembering their mother. And* **Louise**, *who has matured, somewhat, rescuing* **Marie***:*

Louise   Oh, wait'll I tell you – Marie, Marie: I heard this this morning. You know Mrs 'Chisley Park' who doesn't go out that much – or hardly at all any more? And Mrs Doyle who's about the same age? Two ancients! Well, they were out yesterday, both of them – This's true! And they met on Church Street. 'Oh hello!' said Mrs Chisley Park: 'Oh hello! I thought you were dead!' 'Well, if I was,' said Mrs Doyle, 'I didn't see you at the funeral!' 'But, my dear,' said Mrs Chisley Park, 'you were dead for a month before I heard it!'

They laugh, leaning their heads together, touching each other, embracing.

Did I get that right? (*The words of the story. Then, her belongings:*) Childhood things! Childish things! What do I want this rubbish for? (*Taking most of what's left and dumping it on the fire. Then, going into the house:*) I'll take a last look in here.

Marie   These are the keys, Christy. I've labelled them for you. I wanted to give you a set weeks ago, but the Law says it can't be done until the signing's done. Billy Kerrigan said no, an emphatic 'No'. (*She puts the keys on the garden table.*) D'you want this garden stuff? I've no place for it – D'you want the gramophone? You know you paid over the odds for here? (*She laughs.*) So most of the furniture is left in there and you can have it as far as Louise and I are concerned. I know that's how Mum felt.

Christy   Marie.

Marie   My place over the shop is furnished and all but finished. I thought I'd give it – a try out? – tonight.

Christy You don't have to. (*She looks at him.*) If – Yeh know?

Marie Stay? Here?

Christy Well. (*Shrugs:*) Yeh. (*Then:*) Yeh.

A self-conscious moment between them. A car is arriving, which they register.

Marie Here he is. (*And she goes off to meet the car.*)

Louise The big moment has arrived. (*She is coming from the house to collect her final box.*)

Christy All done now bar the signing.

Louise I'm not staying for it. My big sister will look after you. She knows where everything is – located and et cetera. She's the one loves you. But you're probably too – obtuse – to know it. Are you?

He's not.

In case you're interested, I don't. Talk to her. Best of luck. (*Leaving:*) If you find anything that looks like mine, just – phh! – burn it.

Kerrigan (*off, during the above*) You want it done out here?

Marie (*coming in with* **Kerrigan***; to* **Louise**) Are you not staying for –

Louise (*without stopping; mock gaily*) No! (*Off.*) No!

And her car drives away during the following.

Kerrigan's *pride has been compromised. He feels corrupted and he is bitter and angry. And impotent. So, he's talking nonsense. He refuses to look at* **Christy**.

Kerrigan You want the signing done out here?

Marie Yes. And when it's done I thought we'd mark the – occasion? – with a drink under the tree.

Kerrigan Are you sure?

She thinks he's joking.

Are you sure?

Marie   What?

Kerrigan   That you want the signing done at all?

Marie   I don't understand you.

Kerrigan   That it's the right thing to do?

Marie   Is there something the matter?

Kerrigan   Okay, you summoned me here, you want the signing done, you want it done out here – One thousand, eight hundred pounds outstanding: cheque, bank draft, cash, what?

Christy   Cash. (*A package of money – brown paper bag.*)

Kerrigan   Ah, cash! (*He starts to count the money, distastefully.*)

Christy   . . . How yeh doin', Billy! (**Christy***'s attitude is perverse. He's taunting/challenging* **Kerrigan**) . . . I was never much of a one for cheque books . . . bank drafts . . . [I] Keep it under the old mattress . . . What?

Kerrigan   That this is what your sister would've wanted?

Marie   . . . Is this necessary? (*The counting/his attitude.*)

Christy   Yeh? . . . Some of it is English, Billy!

Marie   . . . Won't you sit down?

Kerrigan   That this's what your mother would've wanted?

Christy   Yeh? . . . All there, is it, Billy? Tell us . . . Tell us.

Kerrigan *gives up on counting the money. He has his briefcase and the deeds to the house.*

Kerrigan   Miss de Burca: As the legal representative of your deceased mother, sign there. (**Marie** *signs.*) Thank you. (*He countersigns as witness. He points to a spot.*) Purchaser. (**Christy** *signs.* **Kerrigan** *countersigns. And is putting away the* *documents.*)

Marie   Oh! Lemonade. (*And she has gone off to the house.*)

Christy   Thanks, Billy!

Kerrigan   The smell, the smell. (*An angry man talking to himself.*) Those documents are dirty now. There's a smell off them. This is dirty property now, bought with this (*money*): And I'm sure if I guessed I'd make a good guess about how it was come by.

Christy   Yeh?! (*Mock amazement; defiance.*)

Kerrigan   I've guesses about other things too, but what happens now? Someone else's honesty to be corrupted, like mine was. Betray someone else's – trust. Hers? (**Marie***'s.*) Break down and cry, tell her – *half* tell her what you did and make her feel sick for the rest of her life.

Which gives momentary pause to **Christy***'s defiant face.*
Kerrigan *dumping the money in his briefcase:*

Or, throw her into the river too? That what you did the night we had you 'locked up'? (*He looks at* **Christy** *for the first time:*) You *fucker*! That I should report what I believe to be true and lose my job over you, is it?

Christy   Yeh?!

Kerrigan   You – *scruff* – back from England! Look, why don't you go and – before we do it for you – put a bullet in your head! (*Leaving.*) Good man!

Christy   Cheers, mate!

In the next moment, alone, he chokes back a sob.

Kerrigan (*off*)   The rest will be routinely dealt with!

Marie (*off*)   Won't you stay and have a –

Kerrigan (*off*)   No thank you!

His car driving away. **Marie** *has returned with lemonade and glasses on a tray. Her frown:*

Marie   What was all that about?

Christy   Ah yeh.

Marie   I think Billy Kerrigan fancies himself, has a bit of a swelled head – 'on'm'. Well, shall we have a drink to mark the – occasion? (*Pours drinks.*)

Christy   Marie.

Marie   Oh! The keys. (*She presents them to him.*)

Christy   Marie.

Marie (*toast*)   To the owner! (*They drink.*) May I? (*Sit.*)

Christy   Marie.

The sun is reddening, going down. They are seated.

Marie   Glorious! Isn't it? (*The evening.*)

Christy   . . . I'd die for here.

Marie   This's where you belong.

She has some papers which she is putting in her bag, one of them is a photograph of **Susanne**.

I used to think everyone was in love with Susanne. Were you?

Christy   Eternally fond of you all.

Marie   She was beautiful, wasn't she?

Christy   All of you.

Marie   Oh well. (*Flattered, but she doesn't count herself among the beautiful. She puts away the photograph and papers. Then her frown.*) Though I still don't understand it. ('*How that accident happened.*' *And smiles at him.*) Oh dear! (*She sees that he's upset. She's caring of him.*) And-Mum-was-very-fond of *you*! She loved seeing you. 'A little soul.' She had us *bored* talking about you. July, three years ago, when you didn't come home: 'Where-is-Christy?' Your birthday – she remembered it. New Year's Eve: 'Is he celebrating, I wonder.' Bored! (*Frown again:*) And she was convalescing well, I thought, and coping with Susanne's death, but then it was as if she gave in, stopped. (*Smiles at him.*) D'you know?

He is close to tears.

Christy?

He rises, moves away to look out at the lawn.

Well, I suppose I had better start making tracks ... Shall I?

Christy, *his back to her, nods ruefully.*

She collects her suitcase and joins him.

Christy   Look at the grass again.

Marie   ... Well ...

They shake hands. She leaves. Her car driving away. **Christy** *standing in the setting sun. He chokes back a sob. He deals with it.*

[*Note:* 'A Little Love, a Little Kiss' *sung by Arthur Tracy introduces and concludes the play. Other recordings by Arthur Tracy can be used for bridging the scenes.*]